ETIQUETTE

CONFIDENCE & CREDIBILITY

YOU AT YOUR BEST @ WORK

BUSINESS INTELLIGENCE PLUS
SOLUTIONS TO STICKY SITUATIONS

JULIE BLAIS COMEAU
ETIQUETTE JULIE
PUBLISHED BY JEWELS PUBLISHING ♥

ETIQUETTE: CONFIDENCE & CREDIBILITY
You at your best @ work
Business intelligence plus solutions to sticky situations
COPYRIGHT © 2013 by Julie Blais Comeau
All rights reserved.
3rd printing -- 2015

Published by Jewels Publishing ❤

Authored and published by Julie Blais Comeau etiquettejulie.com
For permissions, large quantities, educational purposes and customised versions
please contact the publisher and author,
Julie Blais Comeau, directly at: julie@etiquettejulie.com.

All book versions may be purchased on
www.etiquetteconfidencecredibility.com and www.etiquettejulie.com.

Library and Archives Canada Cataloguing in Publication

Comeau, Julie Blais, 1962-, author
Etiquette, confidence & credibility : you at your best @ work : business intelligence plus
solutions to sticky situations / Julie Blais Comeau, Etiquette Julie.

Issued in print and electronic formats.
ISBN 978-0-9920566-0-5 (pbk.).--ISBN 978-0-9920566-1-2 (ebook).--
ISBN 978-0-9920566-2-9 (mobile)

1. Business etiquette. 2. Etiquette. I. Title. II. Title: Etiquette, confidence and credibility.

HF5389.C66 2013   395.5'2   C2013-906859-7   C2013-906860-0

Designed by Cinnamon Toast cinnamontoast.ca
Printed and bound in Canada by Rapido Books rapido-books.com
Back cover illustrations by Anne Villeneuve annevilleneuve.com
Photos of Julie by Adrien Duey adrienduey.com

To my parents and grandparents, your unconditional support, gentle guidance, enduring patience and all of your impromptu life lessons have inspired me to teach.

Thank you for allowing me to be me to follow my path from gauche-girl to gaffe-proof teacher with my head held up high.

With tender love and deep gratitude,

Julie

GRATITUDE

Even for a solopreneur used to creating alone with her thoughts and computer, the writing of a book does not happen without collaborations, synergies and synchronicities.

As a first-time author, I have been blessed and blissfully accompanied by the generous gifts of many.

I am sincerely appreciative for the sequence of events on this book's journey. All along my way, the right people appeared at the right moment. Sometimes, it was a whisper and sometimes it was a shout. To me, they were all star aligned moments that made my vision come true.

Foremost, I would like to thank my husband Richard Comeau, my perfect proof-reader. Thank you for having more faith in me, than I sometimes do. Thank you for your love. I love seeing me through your heart. Thank you for giving me the peace and freedom to grow as a woman, a mother, an entrepreneur, and now author.

Thank you to our sons Christopher Joseph and Alexander Jean, my first readers. Your questions and interrogations have kept my writing real. I am a better author and person because of you.

Thank you to my family members; near and far, I always know that you are present. You are a part of me. Your belief and support energize me. I love you.

Thank you to my friends for your encouragement. You kept me going with your sideline cheers and belief. Yeay!

Thank you to *Salut Bonjour*! and the comfort of your set. You made me say it "I am writing a book."

Thank you to Joane Duquette, for calling me on it and for our weekly mutual coaching sessions on Skype. You are next to publishing your book!

Thank you to Janet Wilson, *Ottawa Citizen's* Life and Style Editor, for believing in me and in the power of etiquette. You gave me my first writing gig! Your natural grace is exemplary.

It's a pleasure to contribute to the *Huffington Post Canada* with my *Sticky Situations* blog under the leadership of contributing editor, Danielle Crittenden and her successors. Thank you Danielle for helping me to find my writing voice, for endorsing this first book and for referring me to Susan Ponting – and thank you Susan for pushing me to write my stories with poise. You got it all: the book's mission, its vision and me.

Thank you to Bronwyn Mondoux and her Cinnamon Toast team for creating the visual of this book.

Thank you Sam Clusiau-Lawlor, visual graphic guru. This second edition rocks because of you.

Thank you to Patricia Latour and the entire team at Imprimerie Gauvin, you are true professionals.

Thank you to my clients, media contacts, the participants in my training activities and to the public, for your trust and confidence. You have kept me on my toes and in constant evolution, while seeking the answers to empower you. I am at your service.

Thank you to Synergize Mastermind™, my esteemed international colleagues of experts, my etiquette friends. Our synergy is precious, enriching and stimulating.

Thank you to all the beta readers who came out of my Facebook want ad and LinkedIn connections or who volunteered: Sylvie Castonguay, Judy Campbell, Carrie Cormier, Jodi Leblanc, Wendy Mencel, Sylvie Mercier, Tony Priftakiz, Lyne Ratté, Douglas Trapasso, Renata Uresti Gonzalez, Angela Vanikiotis and Liz Yong. Your guidance was a delightful surprise. The gift of your time with fresh critical eyes, has confirmed my faith in Ask and you shall receive, even from complete strangers. Wow!

Thank you to Lucie Gendron, for taking the time to read, all of my book, and for endorsing it. The way that you 'knit' your career and make connections is simply amazing. I am very grateful for your support.

Last but not least, to all the authors in my life, thank you for the inspiration: Chantal Binet, Martin Blais, Maryse Blais, Kathy Buckworth, Julie Doyle, Danielle Guérin, Jadrino Huot, France Hutchison, Linda Leclerc, Rachel Leduc, Patrick Leroux, David McColl, Peggy McColl as well as Danièle St-Denis. You preceded me into it and graciously demystified it; the writing cave. Now, because of you, I see the light that has welcomed me into the authors' community.

With warm gratitude, love and hugs,

Julie

TABLE OF CONTENTS

TABLE OF CONTENTS

TABLE OF CONTENTS

TABLE OF CONTENTS

LEGEND FOR THE PICTOGRAMS

ETIQUETTE: CONFIDENCE & CREDIBILITY has pictograms to enlighten your reading. Here's how they will guide you:

Glasses share studies, surveys, statistics, quotes or origins to support the facts.

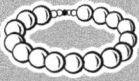

Pearls of wisdom give you practical suggestions, tips, tricks, and what you should focus on in your business interactions. They are based on my experiences.

The cell phone details solutions to contemporary business sticky situations.

Activities, memory aids and templates, that may be photocopied, are identified by a shaded area like this one.

Summaries and chapter takeaways are identified by a shaded area and border like this one.

CAREER VISION ACTION PLAN

DREAMS

Use this page to write, doodle, insert or even glue
clippings related to your career vision.

Are you ready? Let's get started on getting you the career of your dreams!

Excerpt from ***ETIQUETTE: CONFIDENCE & CREDIBILITY***

THE MAKING OF AN ETIQUETTE EXPERT AND OF HER BOOK

| WHO IS ETIQUETTE JULIE?

I was not born rich, or naturally elegant. In fact, at one time you could have even called me gauche! I did not marry royalty either, even though my husband is my true prince and I do hope to live happily ever after.

As a proud lefty, I spilled countless glasses of milk—on average, about twice a week for more than 20 years! I could never throw a ball and have it go in the direction I wanted it to, and, do not ask me to run— while throwing that ball. I have difficulty walking and drinking water while wearing sunglasses!

Yup, that's me.

For years, I researched, practiced, attended seminars, and paid attention to the tiniest and largest of details while studying what to do and say, when and how. As a result, etiquette knowledge has given me the confidence needed to get the career of my dreams—finishing school, or not!

If I can do it, you can too!

As a young student, I was considered a nerd. I hung out with boys and took part in spelling bees. I played schoolteacher in my basement. As a teenager, I started a day camp for the neighbourhood kids in my backyard. All I wanted to do was teach. I still do. I love my job. Thank you for giving me the opportunity to do what I love.

> *Follow your bliss.*
>
> –Joseph Campbell
>
> *Choose a job you love, and you will never have to work a day in your life.*
>
> –Confucius

Because I was marginalized, like many kids, I desperately wanted to learn how to fit in with the crowd. I therefore started to read etiquette and how-to books to appear more polished. I became an insatiable student.

> **When the student is ready, the teacher appears.**
>
> –Buddhist saying

Learning about etiquette helped to dissipate all of my insecurities and self-consciousness, and instead of being dismissed for my awkwardness, I became business savvy and was on my way to building a great career.

Then, just when I thought that I was at the top of my game with a great job as a senior human resources manager, living in a beautiful home, with a wonderful husband and two awesome sons, it happened.

| BOOM! CRASH! & POW-HER!

C'est what? Superwoman does not burnout; she just keeps on going nonstop.

That's what I believed about myself anyway; that I was indestructible, but the pace and pressure of my career life were proof I was heading for a big change, and after a life-changing incident that was a culmination of many things in my life; a visit to three different doctors confirmed I was physically, mentally and emotionally exhausted.

I did not want to admit it though. That was like admitting I was weak. However, sometimes the Universe, or whatever you wish to call it, has a different plan in store for us.

My wake-up call happened on one of my days off. You see, having a day off for me was rare, and on this day, I am not sure if my discomfort was some kind of foreshadowing of things to come, or just that I did not know what to do with myself having the time off, but I felt like I was in a daze. It was so unusual to be able to focus on just me, and to think about what I wanted to do for a change. I decided to go to the mall and went back and forth in my mind as to what route I would take to get there.

Before getting into my car, I clearly remember saying to myself, "Come on now Julie, this is an easy decision, just go!" Still, something just did not feel right to me. A good ten minutes later, I left.

When I got to the first stoplight, I saw a police car speed by me. "Ok, be careful," I thought. The light went green and I slowly turned to the left. Suddenly, from the top of the hill, in the distance, I could see roof-lights flashing on what I assumed was another police car. I yelled, "Oh my God!" I was certain my mind was playing tricks on me, but the alternating headlights coming at me confirmed it was indeed another police car. This one crossed over a lane and was suddenly right in front of me. It was all happening so fast, yet at the same time, it seemed to be in slow motion.

Just as quickly, as the first two cruisers sped by, another car appeared in the opposite lane, this one was white and the two police cars were obviously chasing it.

Moving in the same direction as the white car was a third police car trying to catch up. It was sheer chaos. All three police cruisers then tried to sandwich the white car in. "This can't be," I said to myself, "I cannot die…my children…I have only just begun teaching them. I don't even have a proper will!"

Maybe it was a premonition of things to come, or just my reflective state, but in the days leading up to this life-changing event, I had met with a notary to finalize my will. The thought of it being read coldly, without loving words to my beloved family prompted me to write a letter to my sons, to accompany the will. It would be the passing on of knowledge, from a mother to her children, for all of life's rites of passages, special moments, and even some mundane tasks just in case, some day, I would no longer be here to teach and guide them.

At the time, that document was nowhere near completion. In the midst of the turmoil, in Technicolor in my mind, my children's beautiful smiling faces flashed before me, and all I could think of was the incomplete document on my computer screen. All I could think of, with the cars speeding by was that I could not leave my boys without a "how-to guide to life," and some loving advice from me.

"I have to live!" That much I knew. Time waits for no one; and I knew I had to do something drastic. "Does that officer barrelling toward me in the third car even see me? Julie! Do something now!" It was all up to me.

I looked into my rear-view mirror, and saw a taxi approaching, but it was still far enough behind me ..."I have time... please let me have time!" I pleaded. All of my energies were concentrated in this one horrifying moment. My emotions took a back seat, and my survival instincts kicked in. I had to think of something quickly. Just as the cars were approaching, I regained my composure, turned the wheel to the right, crossed two lanes of traffic and headed into a driveway, which had magically appeared off the busy Boulevard.

I carefully manoeuvred away from the oncoming traffic while hoping that I would be able to get out of the way of all these soon-to-be colliding cars. Suddenly, as I gripped the steering wheel with all my might, jaw clenched, and my right foot ready to brake or accelerate; one of the police cars swerved and smashed directly into the back driver's side of my car! I was pushed to the side while the police car bounced off my car and slammed head-on into a tree.

The officer was thankfully uninjured. I was not hurt either, but as you can imagine I was trembling with fear, and my entire body was shaking. I just kept wondering how all of this could have happened in what seemed like the blink of an eye.

The officer ran to my car and opened the door to help me out. He kept apologizing. More sirens sounded. Police cars, a fire truck and an ambulance appeared. The paramedics checked me out, ran a few tests and determined I was physically shaken and in shock but uninjured. I was escorted to a nearby cruiser where three officers were waiting to question me.

Shaking and in disbelief that I had just survived this entire event, I answered the officers' questions as tears rolled down my face. Still in astonishment, I relived the previous seconds and minutes as I tried to recall the scene from my memory to fill out the accident report.

There is nothing quite like being involved in a high-speed police chase to change the course of your life! Recurring nightmares ensued and haunting questions like, "Why was I spared? What will I do with the rest of my life? Who am I supposed to be? What is my mission?" kept me awake at night, but the entire experience soon gave my life not only a new direction but also new meaning.

I came to the realization that I just could not go on at the frantic pace I was going. I did not have scars or lasting physical injuries from the car chase, but I had time to think, and I soon realized my heart and my mind were not aligned and I was going to do something about it.

What was, and still is most important to me is my family. However, it took this wake-up call for me to realize I was away too much, and I was starting to lose touch with the things and people that really matter in my life. Sure, I was doing it all, but life was not making sense to me anymore.

You have most certainly heard this before, and I would never have said it to myself while I was in the midst of all my turmoil, (looking from the outside to everybody like I was Superwoman), but my burnout was the best thing that ever happened to me.

It gave me the freedom to reconnect with my loved ones and myself and to gain knowledge to be able to teach what I love most of all—to empower people, like you, to be their absolute best.

Within a couple of weeks after the accident, I resigned from my position and started my own business as a training and development consultant.

For about a decade, I fulfilled my role as a mother, took on occasional etiquette and client services training contracts while substitute teaching in elementary schools.

When one of the businesses that I subcontracted for dissolved, I took it as a sign to become an independent etiquette expert, to fly solo so to speak. I therefore enrolled in an entrepreneurship program and built my own business.

| FROM GAUCHE-GIRL TO GAFFE-PROOF TEACHER

How does someone like me go from gauche-girl to gaffe-proof teacher?

On the one hand, it was out of survival, and on the other; it was about following my own true path.

Being a gauche lefty, I wanted to know the answers to overcome my awkwardness and discomfort with people. I knew that if I empowered myself with the right etiquette knowledge, I could display confidence even when I gaffed. By doing the right things in any given situation, I knew I would gain credibility.

My quest was not about perfection. I wanted to connect with people without being paralyzed or noticed for all of my gaffes. I relentlessly sought out the answers to remove my feelings of doubt. If only I could connect in the right way, knowing the right tools to use along the way, I knew I could deliver the goods.

> If you are confident, your mind will be free to focus on the business at hand and more importantly, on the other person(s) and their need(s). Without doubt, armed with the answers to your internal questions, you will be ready to seize the opportunities and present yourself, your services and/or products to the right people in the right way.

I became an etiquette expert by listening to the signs along the way; after the police chase, I rediscovered and reaffirmed my path. My career emerged from fulfilling my own needs and my profound desire to teach my findings and empower others.

In this book, as in my conferences, workshops, blog, and media appearances, I now humbly share tips and solutions for the sticky situations that may arise as you make your way along your own path, and as you create your own amazing career.

Early in the process of building my career, I wrote my business and marketing plans and decided that my advertising strategy would be to contribute to the media as an etiquette expert. My first break came when there was a sudden change of morning radio hosts at my local radio station. The new host needed a team of collaborators, and I quickly put together a proposal. Within days, I was on the air of Corus Radio CJRC every Wednesday morning at 7:50 a.m. doing an etiquette segment that enlightened listeners on the do's and don'ts of contemporary etiquette.

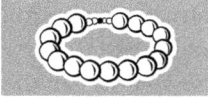

> Write out your career vision and goals including a marketing and business strategy. Look at them often.

> *A goal should scare you a little and excite you a lot.*
>
> –Joe Vitale

The following year, *Radio-Canada, CBC's* French national station, asked me to contribute a bi-monthly etiquette segment. Is it not wonderful how the Universe works? I was already prepared; I had 50 or so different subjects from my former radio commentaries. Now, all I had to do was stretch all of my shorter radio stories into longer TV segments. Preparing my topics for the show's producer and host, I enhanced my original radio topics by adding modern-day solutions to sticky situations. Then, I realized that if I stretched my stories just a bit more I would have articles that I could contribute to print media. I therefore started occasionally writing etiquette articles in *The Ottawa Citizen.*

Just when I completed my TV contract, the new *Huffington Post Canada* called to do an interview on Holiday Office party etiquette, and a couple of weeks later they asked me to blog. Now my popular blog *Sticky Situations* is usually in the top five on their daily posts!

In 2011, after my first official year as a full time etiquette expert, the RÉFAP, a regional community of women entrepreneurs presented me the *Self-Employed Business Woman of the Year* award. It was quite humbling. I am in awe of the beautiful group of entrepreneurial women around me who inspire me.

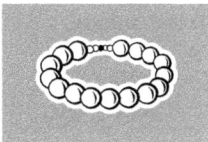

> Network, get involved, join associations, reach out, and meet with people who will support you and whom you can mutually support while sharing successes and trials. Be a listener and a champion of others!

At the turn-of-the-millennium, while I searched for classes in etiquette expertise, I called the Protocol School of Washington (PSOW) to inquire about their *Corporate Etiquette and International Protocol Consultant* certification. I was fortunate to speak directly with the school's founder, Ms. Dorothea Johnson. For well over half an hour, Ms. Johnson and I chatted about etiquette and life in general. She told me proudly that Liv Tyler, the beautiful and sophisticated actress and daughter of rock 'n' roll legend Steven Tyler, is her granddaughter. With an etiquette expert for a grandmother, it is no wonder that the model-turned-actress knows all the rules. Ms. Johnson was engaging and inspiring, but at the time, the fees were way out of my budget, so I put that goal on hold until ten years later.

After two years as a solopreneur, and about a decade after my first etiquette workshop, and that first call to PSOW, I was finally able to attend their courses in Los Angeles and Phoenix and received my certificates. While validating my expertise with official credentials from PSOW, I met amazing colleagues from around the world. I recognized so many opportunities that were in front of me, and for the first time in the School's history, I formed a mastermind group, Synergize Mastermind™, which is now an international network that allows me to serve my clients in London, Shanghai, Sydney, San Francisco and around the globe. Synergize Mastermind™ also enables me to obtain concrete expertise on different cultures from local trusted experts.

> Join, or initiate a mastermind group of peers to share information, synergize ideas and continuously learn about your chosen field.

To this day, I am grateful for my start in radio. I am also grateful for my burnout, and even that horrible car accident. Without these events, and many others, I would have never had my chance to start enlightening the public and getting all the material that I needed to write this book.

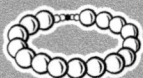

> Recognize opportunities. Realize that sometimes, they may be disguised as setbacks with the purpose of taking you on a different path for your own benefit. Be grateful for your path. It is who you are and you are distinctly valuable.

So now I say, "boom, crash, em-pow-her and write!"

| SYNCHRONICITY AND GRATITUDE

Now that you know my story and my mission, allow me to share a few of my personal beliefs. I believe in synchronicity; that life's unrelated events converge to offer us a chance, a new beginning, or to give us a little nudge in a different direction. It is up to us to connect the dots and transform these occurrences into opportunities. However, like most people, I sometimes recognize these opportunities, and I sometimes let them go. I also know that if something is meant to be it will reappear again in some way, when I am ready.

The process of writing this book has made synchronicity very evident in my life.

For years, I had "it" on my mind. For years, I talked about "it". Many times, I started "it", fine-tuned "it", and then I would let "it" go.

"It" is this book, my gift to you, which is the fulfillment of my mission.

When the year of turning the big 5-0 happened, I remembered reading Julia Child's biography, and that her life as an author of cookbooks and then TV host began at age 50. When I looked over my list of objectives at the beginning of the year, I decided to make a mock book cover.

I pinned it on my Vision Board. I looked at the picture and sat there daydreaming. Immersed in my vision, I clicked away at the draft for my Table of Contents. I pinned that on my Vision Board, too, right next to the book's cover. I looked at these visionary motivations about a dozen times a day and visualized it all. In my mind, I started to think and refer to myself as an author.

The book has stayed faithful to its original intentions, which are to inform, inspire, and educate people of all ages and professions to help make their own career visions come true.

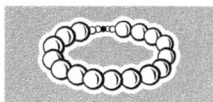

> Create your Vision Board, look at it daily, live it.

> **If you have it in you to dream, you have it in you to succeed.**
> –Alwyn Morris, Canadian Olympic athlete

On May 11, 2012, I celebrated my birthday with my family and friends, and there, in my office, pinned on my Vision Board was my book's layout.

It was the summer of the London Olympics. I received a media request from the most watched morning show in Quebec *Salut Bonjour!* They wanted me to talk about diversity and modern manners around the world. I was thrilled and it turned out to be a dynamic and fun interview. At the conclusion of the segment, the host asked me about my summer plans and to my surprise, I blurted out, "I am writing a book."

Minutes after the interview, as I was walking through downtown Montreal, my telephone rang. It was my sister's best friend, Joane. She called to say she saw me on the show and told me that she was also getting ready to write her own book. She had found inspiration in a how-to-DVD. She wanted to share this special tool with me. She sent me the DVD and the booklet to review, and then jetted off to bike through Italy for a month.

Yet again, it was made clear to me that I had to do it. I said I would on TV, Joane called me on it; and my heart and mind were obviously ready.

On August 1st, after watching the DVD, and doing everything the book guru said to do, I began to write, morning, noon and night, weekdays and even joyfully on the weekends.

The National Capital region of Canada was enjoying a beautiful sunny summer, but I did not get a tan. The only rays I got were those emanating from my computer screen!

Fall arrived and while I was still writing, my speaking schedule picked up, and the telephone was ringing with more radio and TV requests, and all of this in the midst of selling our home. That is another story.

Finally, on November 30th, I wrote the last unedited word to my first manuscript and had what I call my *Little Women* moment. Just like Jo, Wynona Ryder's character, I wrapped my book in a bow. Jo used a cord, and I used a pretty, pink ribbon. I vividly remember watching that scene and feeling the complete fulfillment on Jo's face as she proudly tied her book. I thought, "Someday; I too will have that satisfying feeling of, 'I did it.'"

As I write this, boxes surround my home office. Moreover, as I prepare to leave this home, the birthplace of my first book, I am grateful for the synchronicity of my life and the opportunity to share my hard-won experience with you.

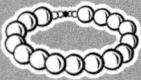

Dream. Envision. Plan. Prepare. Create your own career!

In the upcoming chapters, I will show you how to:

- Take control of your first impressions
- Dress for your client
- Communicate correctly with contemporary technology
- Do not do lunch to eat and drink, but to build relationships
- Network to increase your net worth

The chapters within this book have their beginnings in my radio, television and print commentaries. I also teach these topics in private coaching sessions, interactive conferences, workshops and full-day training seminars.

I guess you could say that I built my business with blocks and elastics. The blocks are the etiquette topics. I stretch each topic, just like an elastic band, to adapt to different teaching activities and media: a 500 word blog, a four minute segment on the radio and if I am lucky, six to eight minutes on TV. For a one-hour conference, I add anecdotes, principles and activities for a half-day session, etc.

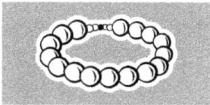

Build your career one block at a time. Stretch your knowledge and incorporate it to grow your career.

Whether you are a career-starting graduate, an award-winning scientist, or a globetrotting CEO, I am honoured that you have chosen this book to educate and enrich your career with interpersonal skills and knowledge about contemporary etiquette. I truly hope that my research and advice on what to do or say, when, where, and what to wear will empower you with the necessary confidence and credibility you need to fulfill your own career vision. It certainly did for me.

KNOW WHAT TO DO AND SAY, HOW, WHEN AND WHY

According to a study conducted by Harvard University, the Carnegie Foundation and the Stanford Research Institute, 85% of the reason people are able to get a job, keep that job and move ahead, is based on their interpersonal skills.

P

eople skills are often called the soft skills. I call them the hard skills. You can have all the education and technical skills necessary to achieve, but if you do not have the interpersonal skills, and emotional intelligence necessary to build relationships, you may never be hired and much less promoted.

Before we get started on the business etiquette guidelines that will give you confidence and credibility, I will define what etiquette is and make its distinction from manners, protocol and ethics.

Many people use manners, protocols and even ethics, interchangeably; and consider all of these as etiquette. These words certainly have business connections, but each has a distinct purpose, and when combined, they will empower you to win in your career.

| MANNERS

Your job is your business, no matter what your position is. Your first few days on the job are dedicated to learning what to say, what to do, how to do it and when to do it.

Manners are the basic standards that apply when you meet others, and they are considered the norm in any society.

Manners are what your parents first taught you as you learned to interact with others. They were reinforced at home and then at the daycare. As a preschooler, when you displayed good manners, you were considered polite. Children enjoyed playing with you because you shared. Their parents appreciated you because you said "Please" and "Thank you."

As you got older, you learned table manners, what to do when eating. You now know not to talk with your mouth full and appreciate it when others also keep their mouth closed while eating.

As an adult, you show good manners by knowing what to do when you encounter others. You keep the door open for a person coming toward you; you offer to help when someone has his or her arms full, and you wait patiently in line for your turn. You practice these good manners daily.

Good manners are about being pleasant and cognizant of others. In my experience, most people are good at manners. They know what to do in most situations. As a citizen of the world, you are expected to display good manners.

In business, you are expected to be respectful and acknowledge others,

The origins of manners, or how to interact with one another, can be traced back to earlier than the 25th century BC.

The Maxims of *Ptahhotep,* is a collection of advice and instructions written in the father to son form, by an Egyptian official. A manuscript copy of the Prisse Papyrus is on display at the Louvres.

A more modern version is credited to George Washington and is now referred to as GEORGE-isms.

In adolescence, the future United States President transcribed by hand, the 16th century Jesuits code of conduct for young men. It is still sold today as *GEORGE-isms: The 110 Rules George Washington Lived By.* [1]

The rules still apply today:

1st: Every action done in company ought to be with some sign of respect to those that are present.

35th: Let your discourse with men (women) of business be short and comprehensive.

98th: Drink not nor talk with your mouth full, neither gaze about while you are drinking.

---

[1] George Washington, *GEORGE-isms: The 110 Rules George Washington Lived By* (New York: Antheneum, 2000).

| PROTOCOL

Most people believe that protocol only occurs in international or foreign relations, but in reality, protocol is all around us; the question is usually when to do things.

Protocols exist to conduct experiments, collect data, determine the order of sequence during an operation; and can even refer to hygiene sequences in certain cultures.

> The word protocol comes to us from the Greek *protos* (first) and *kola* (glue).

You want to stick to protocol for matters that involve hierarchy. For example, you would rely on a country's table of precedence to assign seating at a state dinner. Interestingly, even protocol should be flexible enough to adapt to the ever-changing lists of people attending political, business or social events.

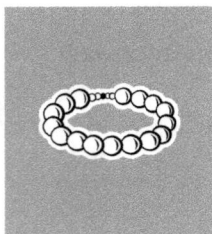

> When responsible for assigning seating for an international delegation, always ask the coordinator of the other country for their order of precedence. Hierarchy, rank and titles may vary from one country to the next. They can also vary from one organization to the next. Hence, it would also be appropriate to ask another company's representative for their organizational chart to assignn proper seating.

Protocols are not exclusive to official conduct in the company of others; they may also apply to some private rituals when you are alone. As an example, if you work in health or community care, you may have a hand washing protocol to follow every time that you visit the washroom, such as:

- Turn on the tap to warm water.

- Wet your hands and wrists.

- Lather with soap for as long as it takes to sing "Happy Birthday".

- Make sure to scrub the back of your hands and between your fingers. Massage your fingertips inside the other hand's palm.

- Dry your hands with paper towels.

- Close the taps with the paper towels.

- Dispose of the paper towels in the pail by the door.

- Use your hips to open the door and exit the washroom.

If you do not follow all of these steps, even when you are alone, you risk having a direct impact on your subsequent interactions with people, such as passing on a virus, and that could have ethical implications.

| ETHICS

The word ethics most resembles the word etiquette, but certainly should not be confused with it. If you have interchanged ethics and etiquette, do not beat yourself up over it. On a few occasions, even experienced media interviewers have used ethics, in lieu of etiquette, when speaking of my services.

Contrary to etiquette, which considers others, ethics is personal and sometimes they even have to be preserved in spite of others. Although personally based, ethical behaviour can have an impact on others, as in the case of the hand washing protocol in the previous section. If you do not follow all the steps, you risk contaminating others.

Ethics are one's philosophical values. Ethics are the moral compass that guides you and your actions with respect to right and wrong. Ethical conduct is guided by personal and usually very profoundly embedded values. Your motives affect your behaviours.

When doing research on a corporation, business or organization you may have familiarized yourself with their Code of Ethics and in doing so, found reasons why they do things the way that they do.

Picture this. You are interviewing with a company for the job of your dreams. As part of the recruitment and selection process, the interviewer shares their company's practices for the testing of their products. They include animal testing. You are an animal lover. You do not believe in harming animals, for whatever reason. Personally, morally and ethically, you do not believe in any form of animal testing. You now have an ethical dilemma: to work or not to work for this company. The choice is solely yours. This is an ethical decision. Your happiness depends on it.

To avoid such a difficult ethical dilemma, when you research a corporation, business or organization, always familiarize yourself with their Code of Ethics. Nowadays, it is usually easily accessible on company websites. Consider all that this Code of Ethics implies and compare it with your own personal values.

By working for a company that has the same moral compass as you, you are on your way to fulfillment: personal and professional.

If you value volunteering, and your company pays you three hours a quarter for community involvement, you will be happier in your life-work alignment. On the other hand, if family is your number one core value and your job requires you to travel one week out of two, you may soon be unhappy and stressed.

Values generate behaviour. To gain insight into your words and actions, I encourage you to write your core values. For some of you, it may be as easy as listing them. If that is your case; good for you. Knowing yourself well at an early age is certainly an asset and will make your career choices easier.

If you are scrambling a little to identify your values, take a look at the extensive list in the next table. They should inspire you. If you need the definitions for these values. They will appear in cards. To facilitate sorting, print and cut them. Feel free to add to the list. There are two blanks spot but you may add more.

Start by choosing twenty; the ones that you instinctively identify with. Discarding the ones that you do not connect with may be a good way to get you started. Keep ten. Lastly, list your top five. Take it a step further and choose your number one personal value.

This exercise can be done quickly or your may wish to let it simmer for days. You can do it alone, with loved ones and even with work colleagues. The results should guide your career choices and will probably explain why the people in your circle do what they do.

Keep your list of top five values close by: on your vision board, make a note on your laptop, or write it at the end of your notebook. Refer back to it regularly. Especially when making life-work decisions.

When in doubt about professional and personal decisions ask yourself: Is this in line with my values?

The pursuit of authenticity is life-long. The more aligned your personal values are with your employer's, the more fulfilled you will be. Honour your values. Plan and act according to them.

PERSONAL VALUES² SORTER

ACCEPTANCE	ACCURACY	ACHIEVEMENT	ADVENTURE
ATTRACTIVENESS	AUTHORITY	AUTONOMY	BEAUTY
CARING	CHALLENGE	CHANGE	COMFORT
COMMITMENT	COMPASSION	CONTRIBUTION	COOPERATION
COURTESY	CREATIVITY	DEPENDABILITY	DUTY
ECOLOGY	EXCITEMENT	FAITHFULNESS	FAME
FAMILY	FITNESS	FLEXIBILITY	FORGIVENESS
FRIENDSHIP	FUN	GENEROSITY	GENUINESS
GROWTH	HEALTH	HELPFULNESS	HONESTY
HOPE	HUMILITY	HUMOUR	INDEPENDENCE
INDUSTRY	INNER PEACE	INTIMACY	JUSTICE
KNOWLEDGE	LEISURE	LOVED	LOVING
MASTERY	MINDFULNESS	MODERATION	MONOGAMY
NON-CONFORMITY	NURTURANCE	OPENNESS	ORDER
PASSION	PLEASURE	POPULARITY	POWER
PURPOSE	RATIONALITY	REALISM	RESPONSIBILITY
RISKS	ROMANCE	SELF-ACCEPTANCE	SAFETY
SELF-CONTROL	SEL-ESTEEM	SELF-KNOWLEDGE	SERVICE
SEXUALITY	SIMPLICITY	SOLITUDE	SPIRITUALITY
STABILITY	TOLERANCE	TRADITION	VIRTUE
WEALTH	WORLD PEACE	[ ]	[ ]

1. _____

2. _____

3. _____

4. _____

5. _____

² http://casaa.unm.edu/inst/Personal%20Values%20Card%20Sort.pdf

| ETIQUETTE

Etiquette refers to a code of conduct within a certain group, society or culture.

Etiquette occurs when you encounter others and consider their circumstances. Etiquette is based on what is collectively agreeable. Solo, in your office, you will never encounter etiquette practices but you may encounter ethical dilemmas.

You know that you need to greet your new client, but you wonder, how to do it. You ask yourself, "Should I put out my hand first or should I wait for my client to do so? And, what if he/she is French Canadian do I have to air kiss?"

Although you may think etiquette is stiff, it adapts to people, their circumstances and the situation.

When I first started to present business etiquette workshops, more than 10 years ago, I did not address cell phone etiquette, I never thought that I would be getting participants to brainstorm about social network guidelines, and I was just beginning to spread the word about the rules of email etiquette. Today, these guidelines are business etiquette staples in any organization.

I like to say, *"Etiquette is savoir-faire without pinkies or noses up in the air. It is about respect for the people and their circumstances."*

> The most popular origins of etiquette are credited to Louis XIV, le Roi Soleil (Sun King). He was so particular about how to do things at the Palace that The Duke of Saint-Simon, who kept the Versailles memorials, wrote:
>
> 'With an almanac and a watch, you could be three hundred leagues from here and say what he was doing.' The King's day was timed down to the last minute so that the officers in the service of the monarch could plan their work as accurately as possible. From the rising ceremony to the retiring, he followed a strict schedule, as did all the members of the Court, all regulated like clockwork.[3]

A perfect example of etiquette in action during the Sun King's reign could be seen on the Versailles lawns. When the French men and women of nobility were invited to the palace for celebrations, they were greeted by *étiquettes* (the French word for tags or boards that contain information) in the garden. The

---

[3] http://en.chateauversailles.fr/history/versailles-during-the-centuries/living-at-the-court/a-day-in-the-life-of-louis-xiv

pickets had signs with warnings, like "*Prière de ne pas marcher sur la pelouse*" (please do not step on the grass). Louis XIV had ordered his gardener to place these posts on the perfectly manicured grass of the castle's gardens.

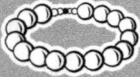

> A good way to sum up etiquette would be the famous saying, "When in Rome, do as the Romans do."

In the privacy of your office, if you have a closed office, while doing tasks that are only related to you, without consequence on others, you will not breach any etiquette guideline. The reason is simple; you are not in contact with anyone. You can loudly chew your gum, eat with your mouth open and maybe even take off your shoes; no one will be offended. Alone, you do not risk breaching any etiquette guideline as long as you are not heard, seen or even smelled.

This book focuses on how to behave in today's modern workplace. It shares correct contemporary etiquette guidelines. To complement your knowledge, it will occasionally address what, when and why: manners, protocol and ethics.

Now that we are clear on what etiquette is let's make sense of how positive first impressions are broadcasted.

SUMMARY

- Manners are what to do.
- Protocol is when to do it.
- Ethics is why we do what we do.
- Etiquette is how to do it.

TAKE CONTROL OF YOUR FIRST IMPRESSIONS

T he age-old saying, "You can't judge a book by its cover" may be wise advice, but whether we like it or not, we are all judged by our covers. It may sound shallow, judgemental and even prejudiced, however, when we meet someone new, we judge everything from their appearance to their body language, and you can be sure that they are also judging us. It is human nature.

Before someone has even spoken a word, we decide based on what we see whether we will like him/her or not. Our perception of other people is deeply rooted in our survival instincts. We function with the fight or flight instinct; and while we are assessing a person, we ask ourselves, "Is this person a friend or a foe?"

According to Roger Ailes, media strategist, president of CNBC and author of *You Are the Message* [4], we only have seven seconds to make a positive first impression.

Think back to any of your most memorable meetings, say the time you met the love of your life, your best friend, your boss, an inspiring speaker, a movie star, or a political icon. What were the good and not so good thoughts and feelings you had when you met these people? What was it that made you decide if you liked them or not? What was that certain *"je ne sais quoi?"*

First impressions in all of your business dealings are incredibly important. Most of my workshops begin with an activity to determine what elements contribute to a positive first business impression. Although the experiment is not scientific, it is solid research with objective human beings. Over the years, I have conducted this study at least one hundred times with more than five thousand participants.

---

[4] Roger Ailes, *You are the message* (New York: Doubleday, 1989).

COURTESY OF ETIQUETTEJULIE.COM

FIRST IMPRESSIONS SURVEY

Take a pen and a piece of paper. Write down your list of the top five elements that you use to evaluate the confidence and likeability of someone you meet for the first time in a work environment.

Make this your own experiment. You can also ask your loved ones, friends and colleagues to write down the five things that influence them most, when they meet a new business acquaintance.

Along the top of the chart below, in the first row, write your name and those of the other members of your study. Then, individually list, in order of importance, the five elements that are associated with first impressions and the likeability factor.

Use the following legend: 1 = most influential and 5 = least influential.

#	Your Name	?	?	?
1				
2				
3				
4				
5				

Excerpt from ***ETIQUETTE: CONFIDENCE & CREDIBILITY***

| POSTURE

Drum roll please! Drrrrrrruuuummmm…. and the Number One element that contributes to sending out a positive first impression is… posture. I bet that it was on your list!

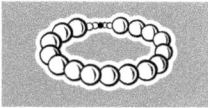

> Mom was right. Stand tall, shoulders back and belly in. Posture is the most powerful element used to broadcast a positive first impression.

Think back to the last cocktail networking event you attended. Everyone was anticipating the arrival of the new CEO of your company.

You catch up with colleagues and maybe have a few hors d'oeuvres. Occasionally, you check the entrance. You quickly dismiss the guests who walk in shoulders slouched, eyes looking downward, or those who seem out of their comfort zone; they could not possibly be the CEO.

Then she arrives, Ms. Power House, your new CEO. You have only heard about her, but you are sure this must be her. At the very least, the woman walking in is definitely a somebody. You can tell. She has it, the X-Factor.[5]

Your mind quickly analyzes what made her stand out from all the others who previously entered the room. Upon closer consideration, you conclude that it is a combination of things, but among the top reasons is her impeccable posture.

---

[5] *The X Factor* is a television music competition franchise created by Simon Cowell. The X Factor refers to the indefinable something that makes for star quality.

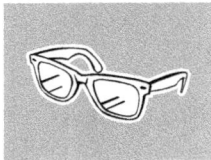

> **Posture. My back is always straight. And I don't make old people's noises.**
>
> –Sophia Loren, Italian actress,
> on looking youthful and beautiful over 70.

THE THREE Cs OF FIRST IMPRESSIONS..........................

Good posture sends a positive message about what I like to call the three Cs of first impressions. When someone is looking at you, they are validating three things about you: is he/she *Confident*? Is he/she *Credible*? And, is what I see *Coherent* with what he/she is supposed to do for me? In other words, what they really want to know is, "Can you walk the talk and deliver the goods?"

Based on your title and your position, others will evaluate the silent messages that your posture says about you. By standing tall with your shoulders back and your arms by your side, you are projecting that you can and will do what is expected of you, and that you will do it well.

I am having a clairvoyant moment. I bet that right now, right this second; you are making an effort to sit up straight. You may even be standing up. Take it a step further. Go look into the mirror, ideally a full-length mirror, and see how improving your posture makes an incredible difference in how you look and feel.

To be in control of your first impressions, you must have a full, top to bottom, front and back view of yourself. A full-length mirror is the best investment you can make to practice sending out positive messages. It will allow you to practice your stance and observe what others see.

When I conduct my Dress for Success workshops, eager professionals always ask me "Julie, I have a limited budget, but what is the first item that I should buy to build my wardrobe?" My answer is always the same to everyone— whether a rookie or a veteran, an artist or a politician, I tell them "Buy a full-length mirror." You need to know what you look like. In addition, you must practice what you want to look like; standing, sitting and from the back.

Seeing your reflection is more valuable than buying an expensive designer suit. You could be wearing a signature blazer and pants, but if your shoulders are slouched and your hands are in your pockets, no one will notice you, and more importantly in the business world—no one will notice what you can do for them.

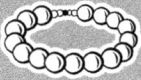

If you do not have a full-length mirror, purchase one. Put it on your list of things to get during your next shopping trip.

THE POWER POSE

Now that you have your brand new full-length mirror, stand in front of it and stand proud. What do you see? How do you feel? Experiment while watching your reflection in the mirror. Try different poses: proud like a peacock, slouching like you have the weight of the world on your shoulders, or even strutting your stuff like you have the world in the palm of your hand. Now, give me your best superhero pose. You know the one—hands on your hips; feet spread apart, eyes looking straight ahead, ready to take on whatever or whoever is ahead. How do you feel? I bet you feel great. Here is how and why it works.

Amy Cuddy is a social psychologist and associate professor at Harvard Business School who has researched the links between one's stance, body gestures, and the release of hormones.

Ms. Cuddy, along with two of her research colleagues, observed hormonal changes as their subjects took on the large and in charge power poses, or the more closed and less powerful restricted postures. The team based their results on saliva tests, which showed changes after only two minutes of power posing. Men and women both felt greater feelings of power and confidence with higher testosterone and lower cortisol (or stress hormone) levels.

In essence, the study concluded that: prior to an important event, in private, standing like Wonder Woman or Superman will give you an edge in stressful situations. If you act powerful, people will treat you as if you are powerful, and you will begin to think powerfully.

So be as big as you are! Do not make yourself smaller. Of course, you would not try to overpower or intimidate someone but simply know that good posture will give you a sense of strength and an increase in confidence.

Controlling your stance has many benefits, so do not be afraid to show your audience your own personal power, and remember to smile!

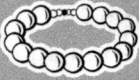

Before going into your next stressful meeting or social situation, try these tips to shift your energy to positive personal power:

- Go into the washroom and take on your superhero pose. Feet flat on the ground and hands on your hips, extend your arms to the ceiling and stretch. Alone in your office, close the door, put your feet on your desk, your hands behind your head and stretch again. Maintain either of these power poses for at least two minutes. Do not forget to stretch out your face by grimacing or smiling; this will relax your facial muscles.

- In a meeting, never hunch over your cell phone or laptop. These positions make you look smaller, like a prey trying to hide from its predator.

- Be aware of your arms. Keep them away from your body. Take up your space without invading your neighbour's personal space.

- Do not cross your legs, once again, it diminishes you.

Olivia Fox Cabane, author of *The Charisma Myth: How Anyone Can Master the Art and Science of Personal Magnetism*[6] recommends to her clients, including a professional boxer, to practice their posture by walking down the street. She recommends experimenting with the majestic Alpha Gorilla pose. More often than not, other walkers on the street will open the way for someone with this pose to allow him/her to continue straight ahead on his/her path. Cabane says the power poses give her clients renewed feelings of personal power, confidence, and a measure of charisma that they did not know they had.

---

[6] Olivia Fox Cabane, *The Charisma Myth: How Anyone Can Master the Art and Science of Personal Magnetism* (New York: Portfolio/Penguin, 2012).

| EYE CONTACT

> *The eyes of men converse as much as their tongues.*
>
> –Ralph Waldo Emerson

We now move to the second place of the top five elements of positive first impressions, and that is eye contact. In your own experiment, you could have a different answer, or have placed it in a different position, but the elements listed here definitely influence how others perceive you—no matter what place they occupy in your top five.

From ancient times when Jesus said, "The eyes are the windows to the soul," to today's young, hip CSI police officers—many know this to be true. Think of poker players for example. Quite a few of them wear sunglasses to hide where they are looking. This way they have all the time they wish to sum up their opponents. With their glasses on, no one can see their eyes blink, twitch, dart, or flutter. Their sunglasses also stop them from connecting through pupils with the other players.

> Pupil connection is what is most often associated with love-at-first sight.

Picture this. It is a regular workday at about 5:30 p.m. Mom just got home. She puts her key in the door and as she opens it, she hears 13-year-old Johnny and 10-year-old Mary quickly running to the back of the house.

"Hi, I'm home," mom announces. As she puts away her coat, purse and keys, she notices that the cookie jar cover is off and on the countertop. She calls out to her children and asks them to come to the kitchen. "Did you eat cookies before dinner?" she asks. "No Mommy, we didn't," they both say, nodding their heads with eyes half shut.

By slightly closing their lids, children instinctively feel safe from connecting with their mother's pupils. If they are not eyeball-to-eyeball with their mother, they believe that half-closed lids allow them to mask the truth.

"Look into my eyes you two, did you eat the cookies?" At which point, when their pupils meet their mother's, they both confess, "Yes Mommy, we did."

It is tough to lie straight-faced to your mother, or anyone else for that matter! In most of North America, from a very young age, we are taught to look into people's eyes when interacting with them. We learn about the correlation between eye contact and truthfulness.

Through eye contact, we are in search of emotional clues, love, lies, and laughter as we also intently listen for signs and subtle cues about the other person. If someone does not connect with our eyes, we feel that we are not being listened to. Think about the times when you are in conversation with someone and suddenly, his/her glance turns to his/her telephone or computer screen. How do you feel? What do you say? You are probably thinking, "Are you listening to me?"

In the working world, through eye contact, we are looking for honesty and transparency. Interestingly, we also give more attentive eye contact to people in authority. We are eager to connect with them or have them connect with us. We all want to be seen, and we all want to be heard. We want personal attention, and our eyes can signal that.

According to the book *The Definitive Book of Body Language*[7], most of us will make eye contact forty to sixty percent of the time. Doing so more often may be perceived as staring, or even downright creepy!

In business, the connecting gaze is concentrated on the upper face triangle. See the white triangle on my face. The base of that triangle is below the eyes and its tip ends where the hairline begins.

The more social glance is an inverted triangle in the lower part of the face. See the grey triangle. The eyebrows are the base, and its summit is the chin. When eye contact is in this triangle, it suggests a more social connection. It could even indicate the desire for a more intimate connection.

If you have ever encountered a lower triangle look from someone in a business situation, you probably felt uneasy and wondered what message the other person was trying to send to you. On the other hand, if the lower triangle look happened in a social or romantic setting, it may have been a nice feeling. It all depends on your feelings towards the other person and the perceived intentions you think they have towards you.

---

[7] Barbara Pease and Allan Pease, *The Definitive Book of Body Language* (New York: Bantam 2006)

As professionals in the era of globalization and social media, we can all now connect instantly, with people throughout the planet. Our colleagues and clients come from a variety of cultures. In our highly diverse business world, there are differences in cultural traditions that arise and we need to recognize them. In some cultures and work environments, eye contact between the sexes, ranks or ages may not be comfortable or even appropriate. Observe, find out and adjust.

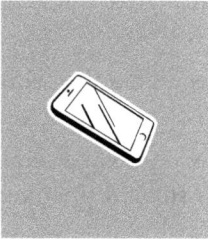

Whatever the reason that eye contact is avoided in business situations, do not take it personally, take it professionally and attribute it to the diversity of our global village. Remember this difference the next time you interact with that person, and follow their lead by looking more generally at their face, and contrary to what you may have learned at an early age, do not look straight into their eyes.

| SMILE

Thus sang the inventive trumpet player and soulful singer Louis Armstrong in his signature deep, warm, jazz-filled voice. These famous lyrics still ring true almost a century later, even in business.

There is no doubt that people want to be respected in business but they also prefer to conduct business with people they like and who like them.

When you smile, you are displaying a positive personality. It does not matter where you are in the world or who is the recipient of your smile. A genuine smile is the one biological form of expression that is universally welcoming, accepting, friendly, understanding, and supportive. It means that you are approachable. It is a wonderful feeling to know you can make a genuine connection with a total stranger anywhere in the world, with a simple, genuine smile.

Of course, a fake or forced smile will have the complete adverse effect.

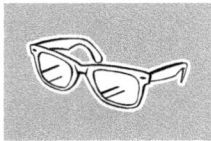

There are health benefits to smiling. Studies reveal that smiling reduces stress, brings higher mental clarity, and boosts the immune system. It may even result in a longer life!

One of the most powerful things I learned from Anthony Robbins' book, *Awaken the Giant Within: How to Take Immediate Control of Your Mental, Emotional, Physical and Financial Destiny*[8] is that our minds do not make the difference between something that we have envisioned and something that actually occurred in reality. Whether a mere fantasy or a real event, we have truly lived both experiences. As Albert Einstein said, "Imagination is more important than knowledge." When we imagine it, we have done it. So go ahead and smile in your mind and in your greetings; it will always make a difference.

---

[8] Anthony Robbins, *Awaken the Giant Within: How to Take Immediate Control of Your Mental, Emotional, Physical and Financial Destiny* (New York: Free Press, 1992).

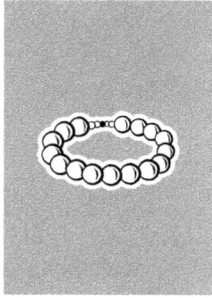

Before you go to your next networking event, to make a presentation, or to prepare for any other activity where you need to appear friendly, put yourself in a "I feel good" and empathetic disposition. In other words, put your mind in a good place. Think of the last happy moment you had—say, on the beach with a loved one, watching a movie and eating popcorn with your family, or singing in the car with the windows open after a fresh rain shower. Feel the goodness of a wonderful memory.

Like the athlete who visualizes every movement in its finest detail, fully experience the event. Feel how your happy memory affects all of your senses. In your mind, re-enact the sights, the sounds, the smells, the tastes, and the sensation of your positive recollections. Now you are ready to go with a natural smile!

An honest smile lights up the entire face and uses the muscles around the eyes. It also usually shows your teeth, relaxes the other person, and opens up a completely new world of communication.

Smiling is probably the simplest and most effective action of business communication. Use it and enjoy—and remember, it is contagious! Make yours viral! You and the recipients of your smiles will feel better overall.

| SHAKE HANDS

Let us travel back for a moment to medieval times. We are knights in shining armour, and we are traveling the world in the quest of conquering new land. We meet our opponents, and to conclude our greeting; we remove our gauntlets for the ceremonial handshake.

However, before we do so, we use our right fingers to bring up our visors briskly (the origin of the salute), to look into each other's eyes and show respect.

The reason we mutually put our right hand out is because most knights are right handed. That is our hand of choice for using the weapons: daggers and swords that are attached to our belts.

We shake hands a couple of times to indicate that we do not have any hidden weapons up our sleeves.

This simple, universal greeting is still the press corps' most prized photo opportunity when leaders meet. It announces intentions of transparency.

I remember my first handshake well. It was in the fall of 1967; I was five-and-a-half-years-old. Dad's boss was coming over for dinner, and he wanted me to make a good first impression.

He told me that the right way to greet a businessperson was to shake hands. He was, and still is, 100% right. The handshake is the universal business greeting of choice.

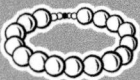

The 7 Ss of Handshaking:

- Stand up
- Smile
- Show the palm of your hand
- Straighten your thumb
- Steady eye contact
- Shake a couple of times
- Slip free

In business, the client or if no client is present, the most senior person extends his or her hand first. In a social situation, the woman or the eldest person extends their hand first.

STAND UP ....

To demonstrate this, my dad took me to a full-length mirror and centered me into position. I was wobbly and felt disjointed. Tall and proud did not come naturally for me.

Actually, most human beings will tell you that standing, arms by their sides, is an uncomfortable position, especially during a networking activity. Although it seems like the most natural of human positions, most feel vulnerable.

People generally prefer to keep their hands busy with a drink or munchies. Others keep them in their pockets, or comfortably crossed. Some may even use them, to camouflage their bellies. There are even some that stand guard like the sentries outside of the Governor General of Canada's gate. And you, like I, know of a few that take on the Adam position; hiding their private parts. Did I make you smile? Good. I am now confident that you will never take on any of these positions, while attending one of these events.

Next time you watch the news, observe the body language of our current political leaders or those of your favourite movie stars. They effortlessly stand with impeccable posture with their arms and hands by their side. That stance did not come naturally to them either.

Like all difficult things that seem effortless in life, good posture can be learned and definitely should be practiced, anywhere, anytime.

Start now as you go to your fridge to get a snack or walk down the hall to go to the staff lounge to freshen up your cup of coffee. Shoulders back, head up straight, action!

Exceptions to standing, while shaking hands include when it may be unsafe as when squished behind a chair or a table, or when someone is physically impaired. In addition, of course, the elderly may remain seated when shaking hands as they greet someone.

When unable to stand, just lean in; bow from the torso upwards.

To help me remember to display good posture, I use "Belly in." These two words echo through my mind and my body goes into action—shoulders back, arms by my side, look straight ahead, and never forget to smile.

SMILE

This is a universal must. No matter where you are in the global business arena, you can never go wrong by smiling.

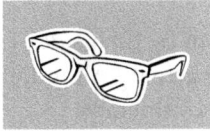

> **Smile and the world smiles with you, cry and you cry alone.**
>
> –Stanley Gordon West, *Growing An Inch*

SHOW THE PALM OF YOUR HAND

Present the inside of your palm, to send out an intention of service and goodwill. Revealing your palm is also interpreted as a sign of honesty, as explained earlier in the origin of the handshake.

It is wise not to show a cupped palm with fingers facing up; it could be associated with the beggar's position that is universally adopted by downtown panhandlers in cities, all over the world.

The opposite, a palm facing down, where you see the knuckles on top, is perceived as a controlling handshake. This is especially true when the twist suddenly happens, at the end of the handshake.

When you place your palm sideways with your thumb straight up, you are signalling that you are on the same level as the other party. You are demonstrating a universally understood sincere greeting of equality.

STRAIGHTEN YOUR THUMB

I am a lefty, so as you can imagine, doing anything with my right side generally feels awkward. When dad told me to straighten my thumb and make an "L" with my right arm, I automatically looked down to make sure that I was doing it correctly. Looking down made my thumb turn downward. I felt unbalanced.

Dad was teaching me the art of the handshake in front of the mirror, so I had a full view. He gently twisted my thumb back up. He had me look into the mirror, not at my body but at the "L" shape that my elbow made.

Forty-five plus years later, thanks to my dad's handshake coaching session, I can always predict a bad handshake—a right hand going to make contact with its thumb down or to the side. That is when you slip and slide.

Remember, thumbs up straight will guarantee, to both shakers, a balanced and solid handshake.

STEADY EYE CONTACT

As we discussed earlier, most of us are very uncomfortable with shifty eyes. During your handshakes, keep your eyes focused without staring.

SHAKE A COUPLE OF TIMES

"Take my hand with all of your fingers, and go all the way in," my dad said as he pointed to my right hand—the area where the thumb and the index meet. "Shake with an up-and-down motion a couple of times while keeping your thumb up."

As we continued practicing, dad added, "Keep your hand straight and don't be afraid to look at the person you're greeting, straight in the eyes," he said, "And always remember that you are a Blais."

I will never forget those words, "You are a Blais". From that day on, I carried the Blais name as if I had been born a Windsor—a member of the British Monarchy's family.

SLIP FREE

This last "S" is something my dad did not address in my private coaching session. I added it after attending a couple of cocktail networking events, and after being greeted by cold clammy hands.

These uncomfortable handshakes are the result of condensation on the outside of cold drinks. It is never a pleasant feeling for either of the parties.

When attending cocktail networking events, hold your glass in your left hand. Your right hand will always be ready to shake or offer a business card.

A slippery handshake could also be caused by nervousness, a hot flash, or maybe even by a medical condition such as hyperhidrosis. Whatever the reason, here are some tips to control a slippery handshake:

Apply antiperspirant (the clear kind) or an alcohol-based antibacterial gel prior to shaking hands.

Keep a tissue in your pocket and gently squeeze it before shaking hands to absorb the extra moisture.

Sparingly add powder to a tissue and once again squeeze your hand around it prior to connecting.

Remember that all handshakes leave an impression: good, bad or puzzling. Make sure that you always leave a positive impression with your handshake, one that is in line with who you are and what you want to broadcast.

Queen Elizabeth II is a pro at handshaking. At 84 years old, in the year of her Diamond Jubilee reign in 2012, she appeared at 444 events and shook a minimum 44,000 hands.

| SOLUTIONS TO STICKY HANDSHAKE SITUATIONS

THE CRUSHER SHAKE ....

We have all experienced this one, and it is not too pleasant, especially if the person shaking the hand is big and you are wearing a large cocktail ring. Am I right, ladies? The person reaches out to shake your hand, and suddenly your fingers get tightened in a grip. They throb. This handshake is usually perceived as aggressive, nervous or in search of power.

Giver: Adjust your handshake to the other party's. If the other party is smaller than you, loosen your grip. Easy and firm does it.

Receiver: Release your hand a little by gently spreading your fingers to expand your grip.

THE OOPS THERE IT GOES SHAKE ....

Somehow, instead of connecting in the middle, your hand ends up a bit to the left or to the right.

Giver or receiver: Start again by saying something like, "Let's give that another try. I am sure we can do better."

THE POLITICIAN SANDWICH SHAKE ....

At the end of what you felt was a completed hand-shake, the left hand of the other party layers on top of your right hand. It is an added gesture to conclude the greeting ritual. Your right hand finds itself in the middle of the other person's two hands. You are sandwiched.

Giver: Use this technique very sparingly. Most people will feel trapped in this handshake. On occasion, sparingly and with close contacts, when you truly appreciate seeing someone, this can be an appropriate handshake. When it is sincerely gestured, it will most likely be interpreted as sympathetic and will be very appreciated, as in the case of offering condolences.

Receiver: Look for authenticity in the other party by observing other non-verbal cues such as eye contact.

THE BABY BURPER SHAKE

This is a close cousin to the Politician Sandwich shake. It is also the favourite handshake of many politicians. Instead of sandwiching with his left hand, the Baby Burper places his left hand on the other party's right shoulder or back and then pats a couple of times, as if burping a baby.

Giver: Avoid this handshake. Some people may feel that they are being patronized.

Receiver: Do not get too annoyed, the shaker probably means well. President Barack Obama has made this his signature handshake. I have not had the privilege of shaking hands with the 44th President of the USA, but I am sure that the intention behind his pat (burp) is to put people genuinely at ease. When I imagine myself meeting him, I can hear him say, "Now, now, don't worry. Yes, I am the President of the United States. Everything is going to be OK Julie, don't worry."

THE SLIPPY SHAKE

The palm is moist, and the fingers are limp. This handshake could be perceived as a lack of confidence or a lack of interest.

Giver: Practice firming your handshake with people you trust. If your hands tend to be clammy or sweaty, read ahead for solutions to keep your hands dry.

Receiver: Look at the other party's face for non-verbal cues. A slight wince could indicate pain from recent hand surgery, or a malaise caused by arthritis. It could also indicate a lack of self-confidence or nervousness especially when you detect red or flushed cheeks and/or neck. Sweating on the eyebrows could be associated with hyperhidrosis. Do not put all your judgement of a person in their handshake. Again, observe all non-verbal signs.

THE PUMPER SHAKE

The shaker keeps on pumping your right hand and never lets it go.

I have this vivid image of my paternal grandfather Romeo. His handshake would go on and on because he simply did not want to be the one to let go.

He wanted you to know that he was very happy to see you and wanted to give your handshake all the respect that it deserved. For him, that meant to keep on pumping.

The pumper handshake could be attributed to nervousness or to wanting to show respect to the other party, by allowing that person with the higher status, to first let go.

Giver: Be aware, only a couple of pumps will suffice.

Receiver: Simply, gently, relax, spread and release your fingers. Ahhh, relief… Keep smiling.

THE TRENDY COOL HIP SHAKE

The fist bump is the new trendy way of greeting. We have been through the high five, shoulder-to-shoulder-bump, and even hands clasped in a classic arm wrestle grip. These are the most up-to-date greetings of choice when the cool kids meet.

Between the time that I am writing this chapter, and the time that you read it, there may be a dozen or so new moves among young people to show respect when they meet someone new.

Giver: Know the other party. Also take the occasion and location into consideration. This greeting may be uncomfortable for someone who prefers the classic right hand grasping shake.

Receiver: Have fun! Follow along and if you do not know the moves, simply smile and ask about the new handshake moves. Be aware, this handshake could also be used by a germaphobe like the self-admitted obsessive-compulsive Toronto born Canadian comedian, Howie Mandel, who fist bumps everyone.

THE DAMSEL IN DISTRESS SHAKE

Once upon a time, when women were not considered equal in business, a lady would present the tip of her fingers for the baise main or a gentle fingertip squeeze by a man. Some older women still present their hands in this way.

Giver: Unless you are in a position or situation where you expect your hand to be kissed, present your full hand, and shake web-to-web.

Receiver: Gently shake the hand presented to you. Do not kiss the hand. Never force your palm past the person's fingertips.

THE NO CONTACT SHAKE ....

Other cultural and religious communities do not allow men to shake hands with women. When you experience this, do not take it personally; it is simply a difference in culture.

Giver: If you are not able to, or do not wish to shake someone's hand, simply say something like, "It is very nice to meet you, I do not mean to be rude but I cannot shake hands with you." You can also place your right hand on your heart and/or add a mini-head-bow. Others will just tilt their head while keeping their hands by their side. If you have a cold or the flu, you can say, "I am a little under the weather so it is probably best not to shake hands". The receiver will probably be thankful to you!

Receiver: Try not to take any kind of rejection of your handshake personally. Move on. If this happens more than a couple of times with someone, do not offer to shake hands with that person again.

| SOLUTIONS FOR NO SHAKE HANDSHAKES

You can tilt your head into a mini bow and place your right hand over your heart.

Saying, "I am a little under the weather, so it is probably best not to shake hands," is acceptable at any time that you do not wish to shake hands. You may be ill or you may be wishing to protect a loved one at home that is prone to illness or going through treatments. Whatever your reason, this phrase is general enough that it will not offend anyone. No, you do not have to give all the details for your refusal to shake hands. That is a personal choice.

When greeting a person who has a hand impairment such as missing a right hand or someone with an arm cast let them take the lead to shake hands or not.

Handshakes say a lot more than we realize about ourselves and about the other person. From your hello to your goodbye—practice the seven Ss to send positive first and last impressions. Master your handshake messages and seek equality not dominance or submissiveness.

| THE FIFTH SURPRISE

The fifth element (or surprise) that usually finds its way among the top elements that compose a positive first impression is punctuality. It is always the Number One key element for any organization struggling with a person's or a team's chronic lateness.

If you are meeting someone for the first time and running late, you may never have a second chance to make a good first impression. Being late shows disrespect for the other person's time. Do not be late!

Other elements that regularly make it in the top five elements for a positive first impression include clothing, accessories and grooming. I will address these in the next chapter, *Dress for your client*.

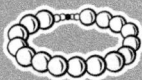

If you know that you have a tendency to be late, here a few tips:

- Whether you are going by car, train, bus or subway, do the route ahead of time. Make sure your practice run takes place at the same time of day as your upcoming appointment.

- In your estimate for getting there, consider traffic, weather, construction, parking and even the elevator traveling times.

- If you are driving, do not fully rely on your GPS. Ask the person you are meeting about their traveling experience to the destination. Be prepared for the unexpected, like a detour. Do an Internet search to seek an alternate route and print it so that you have it if it is needed. Technology is great, but sometimes, when you need it most, it may fail you.

- Call the establishment's reception and ask for directions or visit their website.

- Double up your estimated travel time, especially if you have never been to the area before.

- Plan to arrive early and reward yourself with your favourite non-alcoholic drink and treat. For me, that would be a half-sweet vanilla latte and a mini cake. Delicious!

Remember one of the keys to fine etiquette is, "When in Rome, do as the Romans do." In most of North America, being punctual means that if you and I agreed to a meeting time of 10:00 a.m., you show up for 10:00 a.m.

Showing up early and you may catch your new contact at an inconvenient time, or unprepared.

Showing up five minutes ahead of schedule is acceptable, just as being five minutes behind is tolerable.

When you are ahead of time and greeted by a receptionist, let him/her know that you are early and make a polite request not to be announced until the exact meeting time.

You may wish to take this time to freshen up. Ideally, you would do so at another venue such as a coffee shop.

You can also take this extra time to make an impromptu call. Stevie Wonder had it right; "I just called to say I love you" is sure to make someone's day while having the bonus of putting you in positive spirits.

You usually know about 30 minutes to an hour before that you are going to be late. As soon as you know you will not be on time, advise the person you are meeting, and remember to overestimate and under arrive. What does that mean?

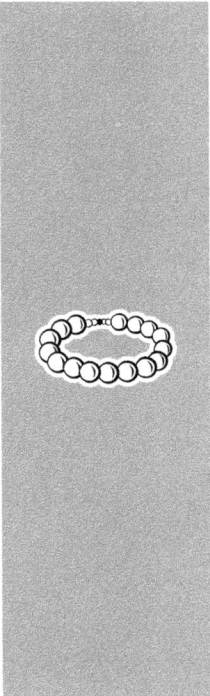

Over-estimate and under arrive is inspired from the wise business advice to always under promise and over deliver.

As soon as you become aware that you will be delayed, inform the other party. Calling is the best method of communication for this situation. Sending an email could be a good backup, if you have previously used this method of communication with the person. Texting should also only be used if you have a history of texting with the person.

For example, you are 15 minutes behind schedule. Call to inform that you will be there in 30 minutes.

When working out the time it will take to travel to your meeting place, make sure to add a sufficient cushion to cover up for unexpected delays like traffic. This way, when you arrive at your destination, before your new arrival time, it will be a welcome surprise.

On the other hand, short change the time and get there past your new arrival time, and you may now have to deal with a slightly peeved or even frustrated person.

When you arrive, apologize: "I am so sorry about my delay." Give a brief explanation. There is no need to go into personal details.

Over-estimate and under arrive is also a good way of setting yourself up for success in all of your professional endeavours.

When using this technique for deliverables, such as working in team collaborations, be realistic about the time you take to complete tasks. Always buffer a certain amount of time to set yourself up for success.

For example, if it usually takes you three days to prepare a client analysis, give yourself four days. This way, you will still be able to accommodate last minute requests from other team members and make the deadline, without having to go into a panic mode.

As a bonus, when you deliver your work under its expected due date or time, because you allowed for that extra time, you are sure to hear something like, "Wow! What a pleasant surprise. I knew I could count on you."

Simply stated, punctuality is a basic expectation that shows respect. In business, late is late. There is no such thing as fashionably late.

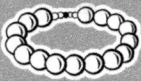

As an employee in today's global workplace:

Make sure to verify your client or colleague's time difference when making appointments. Include all time zones in the appointment information.

Be aware that different cultures may have different punctuality standards. For example, in Germany punctuality is very serious. Appointment times are firmly adhered to. By contrast in Brazil, expect tardiness. Prepare to wait by bringing work or reading material.

A great source for more information on the cultural diversity of the contemporary workplace is the book *Kiss, Bow or Shake Hands: The Bestselling Guide to Doing Business in More Than 60 Countries*[9].

---

[9] Terri Morrison and Wayne A. Conaway, *Kiss, Bow or Shake Hands: The Bestselling Guide to Doing Business in More Than 60 Countries*, Second edition, illustrated (Massachusetts: Adams Mediavon, 2006).

FIRST IMPRESSIONS SELF-EVALUATION AND ACTION PLAN

Take a moment to evaluate yourself on how you broadcast the top five elements that contribute to positive first impressions.

Write down what you do well, what you wish to improve on and make sure to include what you need to stop doing.

To broadcast a positive impression every time, be sure to practice daily, and monitor the things you want to stop repeating, and improve on the things at which you want to be better.

Most self-help gurus tell us it takes 30 days to break a habit or initiate a new behaviour. Revisit your Action Plan for 30 days, and adjust accordingly.

Take every opportunity to practice. All occasions are good. Whether you are simply walking down the street, talking to a cashier or the Deputy Minister, shaking hands with the neighbour whom you have not seen in months or greeting a singer backstage, practice. Practice makes perfect.

You can do anything you set your mind to.

Feel the incredible difference that emanates when you make positive changes and tweak behaviours you want to improve. Increase your awareness of the integral mind and body connection. Regularly assess your mood as you adjust your body's movements.

Moreover, do not forget, you are unique! So celebrate how good it feels to be you, and be kind to yourself in all business situations. Take control of your first impressions, and it will shine through in all of your dealings with people.

Excerpt from ***ETIQUETTE: CONFIDENCE & CREDIBILITY***

COURTESY OF ETIQUETTEJULIE.COM

FIRST IMPRESSIONS SELF-EVALUATION AND ACTION PLAN

TAKE CONTROL OF YOUR FIRST IMPRESSIONS		
Element	**Great***	**Needs Improvement****
Posture		
Eye Contact		
Smile		
Handshake		
Punctuality		

* What you do well / ** What you want to do differently or stop doing

After 10 days

After 20 days

After 30 days

Excerpt from ***ETIQUETTE: CONFIDENCE & CREDIBILITY***

We have now defined the first five elements that people consider when meeting you as a new business colleague, client or consultant. They use silent visual and non-verbal cues to qualify and assess you as a whole.

MEHRABIAN'S THEORY ....

According to Albert Mehrabian, an emeritus professor of psychology at UCLA, fifty-five percent of in person communication is visual. More than half of what you intend to communicate will be validated by how you look, and will mainly be based on the five influencers that we previously established.

Where then, do the rest of the messages come from?

Thirty-eight percent of in person communication comes from your vocal messages. Your voice, accent, and tone all affect your spoken messages. Silence and sighs are also part of your vocal messages. In business, the absence of sound or the release of tension in a quick breath can speak volumes, especially during negotiations.

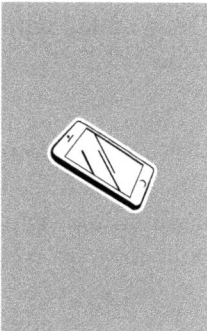

> In times of stress, tone may be difficult to control. Force yourself to speak calmly and slowly. It will regulate the sound of your voice.
>
> Breathing also influences your tone. In stressful conversations or negotiations, regulate your breathing to temper your tone. I know this can be very difficult to do, especially in a highly charged exchange. At those times, it may be best to excuse yourself and walk away to release the tension. Ask to have some time to think about things. Re-start the discussion when cooler heads will most certainly prevail.

The volume of our voices is very influential. Leaders rise and lower their voices to motivate, command, direct, instruct or calm. Interestingly, a lower voice may prompt others to listen more intently.

> As a human resources manager, I had the privilege of working for the Canadian leader in women's work wear. It was a privately owned family business. The owner was a self-assured perceptive businessman. Whether he was in a private conversation with you, or addressing a room full of employees, he spoke with a respectful, gentle tone. His voice was soft and poised. He carefully chose his words. Because his voice was lower than a normal speaking voice, everyone tuned in, concentrated on what he was saying, hanging on to his every word.

The speed at which you talk, the way you enunciate are also included in what people decipher when they listen to you, your accent and your laughter count too. A little more than one third of the first impressions that you broadcast come from how you sound.

What influence do the words we use have on our communication?

Let us play a word association game! I say, D.N.D. You say…?

If you live in Canada's National Capital region you probably answered, "Department of National Defence." If you have ever worked in a hotel you may have said, "Do Not Disturb." Lastly, if you were up all night on your personal computer playing games, your answer could be "Dungeons and Dragons."

Your answer depends on your situation, your knowledge, and ultimately, your reality. Perception equals reality.

If you are strong in math, you have already added the first two elements of face-to-face communication: fifty-five for visual, plus thirty-eight for vocal. The total is ninety-three. Subtract that from one hundred. You are left with seven. Seven is the percentage of your verbal message, the third "V".

I'm sure some of you are shocked.

Here's a scenario with two examples, to illustrate this theory. You and your loved have a little dispute. You each retire to your favorite place. One; after a little while, he comes to you with arms up in the air, eyes rolling and sighs: "I'm sorry!" Believe him? Not. And two; he carefully looks in your eyes, lowers his eyelids, takes a deep breath and quietly says: "I'm sorry." Believe him? Yes. In both cases, the words are the same. As illustrated, the most powerful elements of the communication are visual, followed by the vocal cues.

Your verbal message includes regionalisms and acronyms plus your precious choice of words. They help to bring you closer or to create a distance. Think about business discussions, which include lots of professional jargon. Those who work in the same field understand precisely and rapidly what is being said. The others feel completely left out without a clue of what is being discussed.

Thus, at times, to be understood, depending on your audience, you may have to popularize your message with more common words.

---

[10] John Gray, Ph.D., *Men Are from Mars, Women Are from Venus: The Classic Guide to Understanding the Opposite Sex* (New York: Harper Collins 1993).

One thing is for sure, communication is only effective when, the message sent by the sender, is the same as that understood by the receiver.

In his book, *Men Are From Mars, Women Are From Venus: The Classic Guide to Understanding the Opposite Sex*[10] John Gray, Ph.D. fills us in on the communication gap between men and women. Doctor Gray recommends that we acknowledge and accept our differences. That is how we successfully communicate and build relationships.

When communicating with the members of your work circle, to achieve successful communication you must consider and accept that there will be differences.

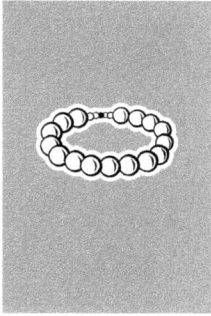

One of the important things all great communicators of the world have in common is the ability to speak concisely and adapt their messages so that anyone can understand them. They can easily explain their theories to a kindergartener or an astronaut. Both the little one and the scientist understand what they are communicating. Successful communication is not about you; it is about the person with whom you are speaking. You need to adapt your vocabulary and alter your references so that it makes sense to the receiver of your message.

Our differences include personal factors. They are the factual societal data that we have at any given time such as age, culture, profession, place of birth, marriage status, spoken languages, and even religion. These distinctions help or hinder our communication with others. These characteristics may quickly bring us together or immediately distance us. These are facts that are out of our control. They cannot be changed.

Personal factors account for a big part of misunderstandings in today's workplace.

Some people are high-energy communicators; others are technical or analytical. Some people thrive in a team, and others may be more productive on their own. You must learn how to adjust to the different ways people work.

Since you cannot control them, it is up to you to adapt your message to make sure that it is well received by the members of your work circle. The more knowledge you have about the other person, the better you will be at adapting your messages to make them relevant to the other person's reality, and ultimately, to successfully convey your message and your intentions to

- Take the time to study and record the top five elements that you use to evaluate the confidence and likeability of someone you meet for the first time in a work environment.

- Think realistically about the positive first impressions that you want to enhance about yourself and what you want to improve.

- Keep in mind the importance of good posture at all times; buy that full-length mirror if you do not already have one!

- Remember the 3 Cs of first impressions: Are you Confident? Are you Credible? Are the signals that you are sending out Coherent? Practice your power poses and make eye contact without staring too long, or completely avoiding someone's eyes.

- Do not forget your own one-of-a-kind smile – use it often; and have fun.

- Rehearse the art of the handshake.

- Be on time for all meetings, whether business or personal.

- Finally, yet importantly, take control of your first vocal and verbal impressions; your tone, your voice and the words you choose.

By being aware of what you broadcast in business, you are on your way to creating the career of your dreams.

Whether you choose to be a doctor, a lawyer, a daycare worker, a financial advisor or an engineer, you will have to make clothing choices that will inspire confidence. Next, we discover how dressing for success in the business world means dressing for your client.

PROFESSIONALISM GUIDELINE #3
DRESS FOR YOUR CLIENT

> *Clothes make the man. Naked people have little or no influence in society.*
>
> –Mark Twain

Whether you are a rock star, a hockey player, a surgeon, or a stay-at-home mom, we start our day the same way. We look into our closets and choose our clothes.

Some people choose based on their moods, while factoring in the weather, and off they go. That is probably what you did back in your college or university days.

Others recognize the power of clothing as being an important contributor to a positive impression. They invest time and energy into shopping and choosing the right pieces. They reach into their closets for the clothes that will have the most impact for their day's activities. They dress for success.

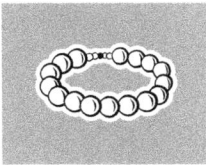

> Dressing for success does not require an American Express Platinum to buy Prada. Dressing for success is dressing for your client, or the client you want to get. Your clothes should also take into account your environment, your client's and the day's activities.

If you are an accountant whose client is Lady Gaga, you may dress differently from an accountant whose client is the head of an engineering firm, or from the self-employed accountant that is meeting with Joe, of Joe's Garage, to review his annual income tax report.

Dressing for your client means that when your client looks at your clothes, he/she knows that you are on their team. What you are wearing should be coherent with what you do for your client. You should look the part to inspire faith in your skills and knowledge. Your clothes should inspire confidence. It does not mean to forego personal touches, favourite colours, or creative accessories. It means to be in tune with what you do and who your clients are.

Even if you never visit a client in the field, you do have internal clients and they should identify what you wear with what you do for them. Internal clients are defined as your colleagues, other departments, suppliers, partners and even sponsors. Internal clients can be found at all organizational levels. They could be hierarchically above, below, or alongside of you. If you are a middle manager, you serve your subordinates in their development. You also serve your superior and other divisions within the company.

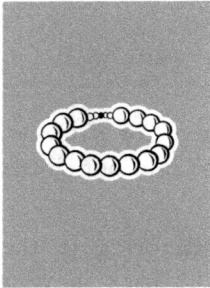

Whether you are a man or a woman, build a professional multi-functional wardrobe that involves:

- Combining ten basic work-wear items
- Knowing your body shape
- Choosing colours that flatter you
- Defining your own style
- Accessorizing for the occasion

| RECOGNIZE YOUR BODY SHAPE

One of my own dressing for success, aha moments came back in the mid-80s when I was a young mom. I was fiddling around the house between baby and chores while watching Oprah. This was back when she was on morning television. On this particular day, she was interviewing Donna Karan, the famous American designer for the stars.

Oprah asked, "Why do you think Hollywood stars like Barbra Streisand choose your clothes?"

The woman credited with the simple chic New York look answered, "Because I understand that dressing people is based on geometry."

I was not the only person puzzled by Ms. Karan's response. Oprah was too. By the end of the interview though, I got it.

Here's what I got. Based on a body's geometrical shape, clothing creates optical illusions. With a garment, we can trick the eye to change our outer contour. For example, with a shorter high waist jacket, your legs look longer. With a belt around your waist, you accentuate your curves, or create the illusion of a waistline. Wear a pin stripped suit and you appear taller, thinner. Aha! I got it. Ms. Karen is an illusionist! More importantly, she accentuates the best in each one of her clients. And you can too; feature your best features with clothing.

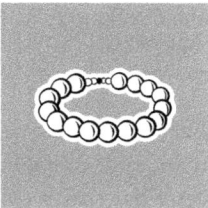

Although there are many variations of the human proportions, in art or even in medicine, the generalized ideal is evaluated at eight equal heads. When dressing, create optical illusions with this goal in mind. Use clothing, to adapt your body shape to this model.
Elongate or shorten body parts by tricking the eyes with attire, colour and accessories.

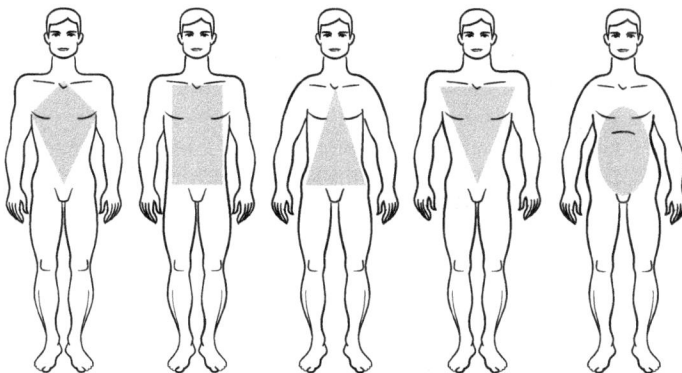

| RHOMBOID | RECTANGLE | TRIANGLE | INVERTED TRIANGLE | OVAL |

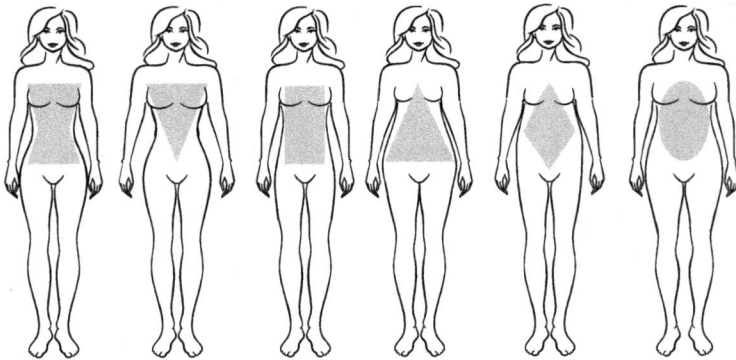

| HOURGLASS | INVERTED TRIANGLE | RECTANGLE | TRIANGLE | DIAMOND | OVAL |

Looking at the above silhouettes, identify your own body type. Memorize your shape and picture it when making clothing choices. Be real. As much as it may be tempting to buy for the body you wish you had, buy for the real you. Let geometry bring out the be-a-you-t-full you! After all, your figure is the basis of your professional look!

Do you remember paper dolls? Children experiment with outfits by folding the tabs of random paper clothing onto cardboard cut-outs. As you shop for

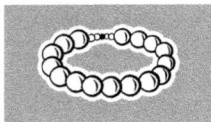

> Fashion should be comfortable. When you are pulling and tugging, you are not looking confident. Confidence will always be the most important thing you wear.

clothes, or match items in your current wardrobe, visualize your shape as one of these figures. Then, imagine the items from the hanger, rack or shelf, tabbed on to that shape. Choose the items that will give you what you want to project, based on shape and color.

Clothing does many things including shape, accentuate, diminish, enhance or deter attention, to body parts. Experiment by trying on a variety of pieces.

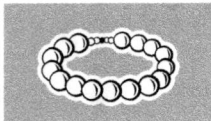

> The choices you make for your attire will direct the glance of others and ladies beware, this does include cleavage and hemlines.

Ask for the advice of the people that you trust.

If experimenting with clothing is not your thing, invest in a consultation with a personal shopper. Most major upscale retailers offer this service in-store. It is worth paying a few extra dollars for a suit to learn about your body and its ideal clothing style, shape and colour matches.

You can also look on-line for an image consultant. I recommend choosing one who is part of the *Association of Image Consultants International* [11] or if you live in the province of Québec seek a *Les Effrontés* [12] certified consultant.

During your customized shopping session, you may discover a particular brand that seems to be custom made, just for you. It could be a house brand or a worldwide chain label. Whenever you put on those items, made by that particular designer, you feel good! Once you find a label that fits just right in the shoulders, the crotch, and the length of the arms, without adjustment, be loyal to it. Make it your brand. It will make your shopping easier, more enjoyable, and much faster.

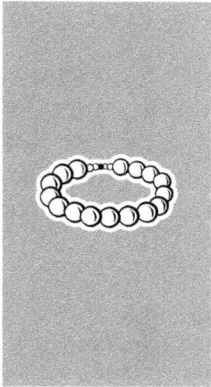

Alterations are the secret to a polished look. When the stars or their stylists purchase an item of clothing, they never look at the size on the tag. They use the measurements from the body's widest parts; buttocks, breasts, thighs, biceps or belly; and buy to match the numbers on the measuring tape, not on the tag. Then, they make the necessary alterations.

If you do not know a seamstress or tailor, call the best men or women clothes retailer in your city and ask them to recommend one. You will never regret finding someone who can do alterations for you. Going forward every item of clothing you own will be just right for you.

---

[11] http://www.aici.org
[12] http://www.leseffrontes.com/en

| UNDERSTAND THE POWER OF COLOURS AND SHADES

What is your favourite colour? No matter what it is, I bet you answered right away. Its' thought may have brought a smile to your face. It makes you feel good. You have probably been loyal to that colour for more than 20 years. You have coloured with it. You choose it whenever you can. You wear it on your back, your feet, and it is the colour of the scarf that covers your nose in the winter. The walls of your room may even be a lighter shade of it.

On the flip side, you may have colours that you do not like; colours that do not make you feel good.

Positive or negative, we all have emotional connections to colours.

Artists, designers, publicists, and even therapists communicate and influence based on the psychology of colours. You act or react based on the feelings that colours conjure up in you.

While colour perceptions are subjective, there have been general meanings associated with them. Black could be class, authority, formality or lack of creativity. Blue can make you feel calm, possibly depressed, but is known as the universal colour of peace. Red can be a call to action, passion or danger. Yellow is cheery, but also fatiguing to the eyes. Colours also have different meanings in different cultures.

> *Everyone has a specific colour palette that flatters him or her, and it is based on eye, skin and hair colour. When you wear colours that are suited to you, it draws people in your direction.*
>
> –Leatrice Eiseman, Executive Director of the Pantone Color Institute

Colours used in advertising and in decoration harmonize and send a message. When you dress for work, use them first to flatter you, and secondly, to influence the people you are going to meet.

Think about it: would you react the same way to person dressed in a mono-chrome brown suit and shirt compared to the person wearing a camel beige suit adorned with a scarlet scarf?

There are many free on-line colour analyses available. The on-line question-naires prompt you for the colour of your skin, your eyes and your hair. Based on your answers, they recommend clothes and colours that complement you. Some of these programs also include the purchase of fabric palettes. These mini swatches of colour take the guesswork out of shopping. Here too, in your quest for your own individual colour palette, the support of a personal shopper or image consultant may be beneficial.

Revisit your colours whenever you change hair colours and every five years or so. Our tones evolve and what made your skin glow ten years ago may now make you look pale.

In business, the goal is for people to look and listen to you; not to pay

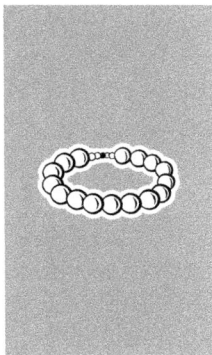

> Although your skin tone, eye and hair colours dictate what shade is best for you; colours that look good on everyone, no matter what your natural skin tone is, are:
> - Eggplant
> - Grey
> - Navy
> - Rose
> - Red
> - Sand

attention to the colour or the outfit that you are wearing. Choose basics in colours that are not too warm and not too cool.

Accessories can be in contrast or in harmony with your ensemble. Fire engine red; pumps for a woman or suspenders for a man, will add a touch of creativity to a classic grey suit. The same suit complemented with charcoal coloured accessories, will broadcast send a more sombre and serious image.

> Your dress for success colour goal is for your best friend to say: "Wow, you look great!" and not "Wow that colour looks great on you!". The second exclamation would be too much of a good thing.

As I explained earlier, colour combinations, just like your shape or the tailoring of your clothing, can create a geometrical advantage. A monochrome head-to-toe look will elongate you. Put a brightly coloured jacket on top of that outfit, and the attention is now on your upper body. Add a fitted colourful belt and you have a curvy waistline. There is no right or wrong answer. It all depends upon the image that you want to broadcast.

When making colour choices pay close attention to patterns. Stripes and plaids are more classical than prints or geometrical styles. Use patterns sparingly, or to accentuate an otherwise bland ensemble with one pattern.

On the other end of the spectrum is a mixture of bright colours and

> As a speaker and television media contributor, I generally avoid busy patterns. The smaller ones give a moiré effect and the larger ones just add another element for the eye to consider. They deter from what I am saying. I usually choose a monochromatic outfit and add a bright splash of color.

patterns, which can make us forget about the whole body and just focus on the person. Think of *Hockey Night in Canada's* Don Cherry. Mixing and matching, or at least pairing colours and patterns is a big part of his brand and it works, for him.

I have to admit that on more than one occasion, I have tuned into *Coach's Corner*, after the first period, just to see what he was wearing. There is never a dull moment with the Grapes (that is his nickname, probably because he always goes on about having "sour grapes")! The former Boston Bruins coach is a recognized hockey expert, and his look is part of his brand. Without Mr. Cherry's credentials, I doubt that he would have stayed on TV for this long, except for an episode of *What Not to Wear*.

Unless you are an established expert in your field, experiment with colours and patterns with care. When choosing an outfit, especially for an interview, go for the more conservative—notice me, my brains, my creativity and my experience, not my outfit, look.

| STAY TRUE TO YOUR STYLE

> *Fashion fades, only style remains the same.*
>
> —Coco Chanel

Unlike dining etiquette, which has many rules, style only has one rule: whatever your style is, stick to it. Your current style may not be forever, but constant experimentation with clothing styles could be quite damaging to your professional image. It sends conflicting messages. Your colleagues and clients will not know what to expect from you.

A common mistake is to swing from one style to the next, or to take on someone else's style because it looks good on him/her. Style comes from within you. Your personality, likes and lifestyle define your style. When all of these change, your style may change too.

If you do not think you have a style, let me assure you; you do. The absence of style is a style in itself.

Here too, there are free on-line questionnaires that will help you identify your style: preppy, romantic, classic, trendy, sporty, etc. In addition, as I have previously mentioned, personal shoppers and image consultants can guide you in this field.

Another style option is to find inspiration in a muse. It could be a character in a television series; a fictional person who has a role and works in a business environment similar to yours. He/she has comparable physical attributes; and their style works with what they do. You do not have to buy the same designer threads, just look at these icons for style inspirations.

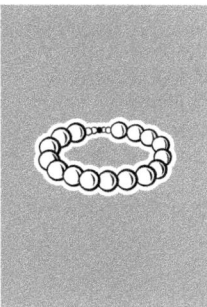

- Style is not to be confused with fashion.
- Fashion is what to wear now, and includes colours, designs, lengths, accessories, and fabrics. It is always evolving and changing.
- Even when fashion trends make a comeback, they are not exactly the same.
- Style is timeless. Your style should always be the same and integrate only fashion elements that complement you.

Think of a private college uniform, boring is what you may be thinking. Everyone wears the same thing. Kids being kids want to express their individuality. They find ways to give the school's uniform their personal touch. An extreme example of this would be Will Smith as *The Fresh Prince of Bel-Air.*

He wears his uniform navy blue blazer inside out to show its brightly coloured lining, loosens his necktie and reverses his baseball cap. I can just imagine all the head masters heads rolling, as this trend took off in private colleges.

The world's most stylish dressers are not necessarily the world's most beautiful men and women. Think of the Italian men's "al dente" (tooth full) attention to details and the French women's "je ne sais quoi" (not sure what it is) panaches. Style setters know who they are and what image they want to project. Stylish personalities include James Bond, Johnny Depp, Jay-Z, Anderson Cooper, Elton John, Michelle Obama, Catherine the Duchess of Cambridge, Emma Watson, and Lady Gaga, they have all spent their lives creating and branding their own distinct styles.

The trick to accomplish your own professional style is to stand out positively while still representing your profession, your employer, and your collective values.

Style starts by only wearing what makes you feel great. Because a fashion magazine says that it is in, it does not mean that you will look confident and credible in it. Suzie or John in HR may be able to pull off the latest trend, but maybe you cannot. Ask yourself "Do I feel good in this? Am I comfortable?"

Do not be afraid to experiment in the privacy of the store's fitting room or at home. Remember to hold your dress rehearsals in front of a full-length mirror. You want to see it all: from the front, the back, the side and from the top of your head to the tip of your toes.

For women only
In her book *Women, Work & the Art of Savoir Faire: Business Sense & Sensibility*[13], Mireille Guiliano, former Senior Executive and Spokesperson for Veuve Clicquot, recommends a smexy: smart and sexy, but not revealing, fashionable look.

---

[13] Mireille Guiliano, *Women, Work & the Art of Savoir Faire: Business Sense & Sensibility* (New York: Atria Books, 2009).

| ACCESSORIZE HARMONIOUSLY

> *The most valuable item in your wardrobe is not a piece of clothing; it is an accessory. With a quick switch of a handbag or a pair of shoes, you can instantly change your look and mood.*
>
> –Donatella Versace

Accessories enhance your clothes and give you versatility. The right trimmings can take you from business casual to business formal, from a breakfast meeting to a cocktail reception.

Accessories should adapt to the season.

Remember more than half of your first impressions come from your visual message, including what you wear.

What can accessories do for you?

Professional Activity	Breakfast networking with IT team at the deli	Brainstorming with colleagues in the office	Sales banquet with Big Boss at his private club
Solid neutral colour classic dress	• Fabric flower at lapel height • Brown leather belt • Matching flat boots	• Gold print scarf around the neck • Gold chain belt • Nude pumps	• Pashmina • Pearl necklace and studs • An evening bag • Nude hose • Leather pumps that match the dress
Solid neutral colour classic suit and white shirt	• Brown belt • Brown penny loafer	• Paisley tie • Black leather belt • Black lace up shoe	• Solid colour tie • Handkerchief • Cufflinks • Suspenders • Black Wingtip shoes

Traditional accessories include bags, belts, shoes, socks, hose, jewellery, scarves, ties and suspenders.

Contrasting hair colours, tattoos, piercings, make-up, motif manicures, and even a flashing Bluetooth are considered contemporary accessories.

Accessories send messages about you. The right additions will professionalize your basics. Accessories are also a great way to incorporate the season's trends into your professional closet.

Your choices for a pen, a notebook or the cases for your technological devices must also be harmonious.

| DOS AND DON'TS OF PROFESSIONAL ACCESSORIES

Have you ever had your colleagues or a client look at you sideways when you show up for a meeting? Could they have thought, "Hmm, did I miss the email for today's dress down/crazy day?"

As you experiment with accessories and observe them in others, you will come to know the accessories that enhance and complement an outfit. You will also, come to know the ones that are distracting and take away from projecting confidence and credibility.

Here is a list of accessorizing dos and don'ts. At the end of each list, I have added extra lines, so you may input your personal favourites.

DOS ....

Invest in a good haircut

When others are scanning you from head to toe, they will assess who you are. Before they look into your eyes, at a distance, they will start to get a sense of your personality from your hair. Is it short and sassy or long and casually tousled? Does it say confident or sexy? Your hair contributes to your brand. Your hair has personality.

> *We now have clear evidence that hairstyle does dramatically affect first impressions and is linked to perceived personality traits. You might even say, projecting the right image depends on creating the hairstyle that is right for you.*
>
> –Diana Shaheen
> North American Marketing Director for Physique
> *An Experimental Investigation into the Effects of "Bad Hair"* January 2000

A bad hair day can have an impact on even the best of us. You can avoid this by getting your hair trimmed regularly and learning a few tips to cope with the humidity of summer as well as the dryness of winter.

Remember to tame the hair on the back of your head. This also applies to you, gentlemen. People walking behind you see your bed head. It is as important as the hair that frames your face.

For the days when you do not have the time or choose not to wash your hair, keep a spray bottle handy and refresh your locks by lightly spraying them with water and then styling.

Wear make-up

According to the American Economic Review, women who wear subtle make-up earn up to 30% more than women who go without.

Large department stores offer seasonal makeovers to present their new collections. It is the perfect occasion to receive a personal tutorial on how to enhance your features and camouflage your little imperfections. All the store generally requires is the purchase of a couple of products. Make sure to let the make-up artist know that you want to create a polished and professional look. Once you have the colour and product suggestions, complete the list of cosmetics at your local drugstore.

Date night #styletip: Keep your makeup natural and pretty, not pretend-y. #confidence is key! #styletip

–Michael Kors Tweet August 4th 2012

Invest in a quality purse and/or multi-purpose bag

Due to its size, it will often be the first accessory on which others will judge you. It is what they will see first. Make it good.

Match jewellery metals

Wearing a silver watch with a gold belt buckle and pewter earrings can be distracting. Metals that match have a more unified, polished look.

Cover an elastic waist with a belt or a scarf

It will take away the reminder of children or elderly wear. Don't show elastic waistbands.

Maintain your shoes, boots and their heels

Shoes protect you and allow you to get from A to B. They are the most functional and important of accessories. Show them the respect that they deserve.

Many people claim that shoes convey information on personality, status, or politics. Ask around. The parallels that are made between shoes and personalities will surprise you. I certainly find this interesting.

Keep a buffer in your desk drawer. Seasonally, have your shoes polished. Replace their heels, as needed. Use shoetrees for seldomly worn shoes—rolled up magazines, or pool noodles, will keep your long boots standing tall.

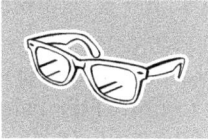

> *Shoes transform your body language and attitude. They lift you up physically and emotionally.*
>
> —Christian Louboutin

Learn at least three ways to wear a scarf

It is the most versatile accessory. Under a blazer, it can look like a blouse. Around your neck, it frames your face. On your shoulders, it adds an extra layer of warmth.

Learn how to make a half-Windsor knot or bow tie on your own

Never, ever wear a clip-on! Like everything that involves dexterity, practice tying your tie. There are plenty of videos, how-to diagrams, and I am certain that dad, grandpa or your roommate will be happy to coach you. You may not wear a tie daily, but the day that you need to, you may be a bit nervous and you could even be trembling…so you will be wasting time. Learn it now.

Use collar stiffeners

It is this kind of attention to detail that gives a crisp, fresh look to any shirt.

Wear suspenders

If you want to elongate your silhouette. Suspenders will make you look taller. On the other hand, a belt cuts your torso in half; it could make you look shorter.

Choose a subtle, neutral telephone cover

Your telephone cover should not attract attention. It should blend in, especially if you wear it on your belt.

Note for women: wear nylons or panty hose instead of going bare legged.

They are flattering. They smooth the skin, even skin tones, and cover cellulite, bruises and veins.

From 2010 to 2011, L'eggs and Hanes reported that in the United Kingdom, sales increased 85 percent for nude hosiery, and Kate Middleton, the new Princess inarguably helped the trend take off.

One of the contemporary public examples of the power of accessories and knowing what, and in this case what not, to wear to influence, was seen in the movie The Iron Lady. The 2011, double Oscar winning, movie looks back on the life of Margaret Thatcher. Picture this. Ms. Thatcher is in front of the television with two of her advisers. They are analyzing her image during one of her candidacy speeches. Like many of her era, the candidate's style is cultured but unlike many world leaders, it is not sombre. Her hair is set in a regal style reminiscent of her majesty Queen Elizabeth II. She wears feminine royal blue skirt suits with bowed blouses, not black pantsuits with crisp white shirts, like her opponents. Polished shoes, pearls, gloves, a purse and a hat always complete her outfits.

To gain the confidence of the people, to make her look and sound like the leader she can be, the two image-makers, ask her to lose the pillbox hats, the pearl necklaces and to change her high pitched tone to an authoritative one.

She implements two out of three recommendations. She keeps the pearls, a sentimental favorite. Margaret Thatcher goes on to become the first woman Prime Minister of the United Kingdom.

As she travelled the world as an American diplomat, the first woman to become the United States' Secretary of State (1996), Madeleine Albright, used accessories, specifically pins and brooches, to broadcast messages of her political agenda and even her feelings.

In her book, *Read My Pins: Stories from a Diplomat's Jewel Box*[14], Ms. Albright shares how she chose a snake pin to meet with Saddam Hussein after one of his staffers referred to her, in the press, as an unparalleled serpent. The book also has a picture of the gold dove, a gift from the widow of the Israeli Prime Minister Yitzhak Rabin, which she wore to speak about Middle East peace.

---

[14] Madeleine Albright, *Read My Pins: Stories from a Diplomat's Jewel Box* (New York: HarperCollins 2009).

Your list of successful accessorizing tips

_____

_____

_____

_____

_____

_____

_____

_____

DON'TS ....

Wear too much make-up

It will make you look like a novice, or a clown, and you will not be taken seriously. Always look at your make-up in natural daylight. Use the visor mirror in your car before leaving home, or carry a small mirror in your purse to do a double take while waiting at the bus stop.

Over accessorize

Twelve accessories are the maximum that you should wear at one time. Bright make-up, eyeglasses, coloured hose, nail polish, etc., they all count. Good models of the appropriate use of accessories are news anchors. They add select few pieces to their generally conservative suits. Their accessories are in harmony with their clothing. They typically blend in. They do not distract and take away from what they are saying.

Wear fake designer accessories

They will make you look cheap. Save for the real thing or buy no name good quality enhancers.

Carry more than two bags at a time

You will look disorganized, like a bag lady.

Wear your Bluetooth indoors

Its flashing light is distracting and makes you look as if you are in a *Star Trek* episode!

Wear your sunglasses indoors

Even as a headband on your head. Leave them in your car or put them in their case.

Wear worn-out accessories

They will make you look inattentive to details. Do not forget about the pen with which you write. Invest in a quality pen. Do not chew on your pen or any other accessory! Do not forget that your professional day timer and your notebook count too. Choose wisely and refresh them as needed.

Wear patterned or fishnet stockings

They are unprofessional.

Assume that belts and footwear always have to match

They do not but they should complement one another.

Wear accessories that make noise—i.e., dangling bracelets, when you are making a presentation

They will compete with your words and actions for the participants' attention.

Tuck your tie in your pants

It looks like your tie is too long or your pants are too high. If you are concerned about your tie flying in the wind, use a tie clip.

Wear suspenders along with a belt

You do not need both to hold up your pants. Choose one.

Wear a polar fleece shoulder wrap to warm up in the winter months

It could be mistaken for a blanket.

Mix more than two patterns

Once again, it is distracting.

Your list of accessorizing faux pas

_____

_____

_____

_____

_____

_____

_____

| LOGF (LADIES ONLY GENTLEMEN FORBIDDEN)

Gentlemen, feel free to skip over this section to go play GOLF (Gentlemen Only Ladies Forbidden) unless you want to pass along the information to the special woman in your life.

Ladies, read on!

> Trivial Pursuit question: Who invented the brassiere?
>
> Trivial Pursuit answer: Otto Titzling
>
> It may be an urban legend, made up by a humourist, but the next time that you play the game, you will be able to answer correctly the pop culture question.

Oprah had it right when she dedicated an hour-long show to the quest for the perfect fitting bra!

Although you wear a bra every day, you may have never invested the time and energy to have one properly fitted. You probably spent more time figuring out the ideal dimensions for a couch than for your bra, chest size and cup. Whether you have a bra muffin top, back cleavage or armpit flab, knowing whether you are 32A, 34B or 38DD, will do wonders for your figure. Every top you own will look better. I promise.

Do not wait any longer; go get fitted. All the retail associates at your favourite lingerie retailer have the tools and the expertise to help you "Salute the sun", as Oprah says, "support the sisters", as many others say. These bra fitters will also help with the choice of your brassieres: strapless, sports or bustier. They all have their purpose in your wardrobe and they all deserve a place in your undergarment drawer.

While we are at it, actually under it, invest in supporting underwear. Ridges are supposed to be seen…only on potato chips, not your bottom or mid-torso. Nobody should to be able to guess whether you are wearing a frilly tong or cotton briefs…unless you want them to, of course. For the rest of the time, your underwear should remain a secret.

> *And the more revealing and provocative your clothing is, the more it can interfere with your performance.*
>
> –Arlene Dickinson
> Excerpt from her book *Persuasion*[15]

---

[15] Dickinson, Arlene (2011). *Persuasion*. Collins Canada

| BUILD A SEASONAL 10-10 S.E.S. WARDROBE

> Every successful wardrobe begins with one household article: a full-length mirror. Before you leave home look at what others will see, from head to toe and from the back too.
>
> *–Inspired by the 2007 PBS documentary MONARCHY: The Royal Family at Work*

Before you land that job, the coveted one, you must effortlessly look the part. It does not need to be complicated. Successful wardrobes can be achieved with the acronym S.E.S. (Keep It Simple, Smart, Elegant and Stylish).

Whether you are a man or a woman, your wardrobe basics start with your interview outfit. As a professional accountant, doctor, engineer or lawyer, working in a formal environment, a two-piece suit for men and a three-piece (jacket, pants and skirt) suit for women is the basis of your professional wardrobe.

If you are part of the arts or of a more liberal business community, a mix and match made up of a jacket, top and pants or skirt, are a sure bet.

It is official; you got the job! Congratulations! Now your white-collar wardrobe, that of a professional, needs to be versatile enough to take you from your head office's penthouse executive boardroom to the local charity's casual Friday picnic.

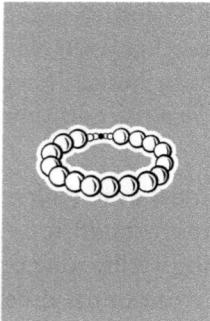

> Inspect every piece in your current wardrobe and only keep:
> - What makes you feel great
> - Reflects your position and company
> - Is in perfect condition
> - Fits you well
>
> Donate the rest; pass it on or save it for your weekend wear.

For functionality, to fit any budget and to allow for self-expression, I promote a 10–10 workwear wardrobe—ten workwear basics for ten days at work. These ten pieces can be mixed and matched to meet all of your day's professional activities.

The contemporary professional man's checklist includes 20 pieces, and the contemporary woman's checklist has 25. You probably are not surprised and

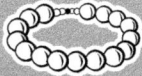

Your 10–10 S.E.S. wardrobe must:

- Respect your employer's dress code: when in doubt, find out
- Reflect your style
- Be clean, stain free and not be in need of repair
- Fit well; not be too big or too small
- Reflect your day's activities, the season and the weather

An accountant would not wear the same thing for a middle of winter day at the office, balancing P & L statements compared to a visit to a dairy farm to conduct an inventory, in the middle of summer.

I am sure that you understand why. Simply put, ladies' wear has so many more choices and options than men's wear. We have the additional options of wearing a skirt or a dress.

On the next pages, you will find the full checklist for your seasonal wardrobe. It includes your basic workwear items plus accessories for every season. After your checklist, you will find wardrobe guidelines, fashion basics and your personal professional shopping information.

I encourage you to fill in your information, photocopy it, shrink it, scan it or upload it before going shopping. It will save you time and avoid making purchasing mistakes that you will never wear.

You can also use *Pinterest*[16] to pin photos and build your seasonal wardrobe board.

---

[16] https://pinterest.com

10-10 WARDROBE CHECKLIST – MAN

#	Basic Workwear	Details: colour, prints, shape, brand, size	✔
1	Suit		☐
2	Suit pants		☐
3	White shirt		☐
4	Solid colour shirt		☐
5	Print shirt		☐
6	Polo shirt or t-shirt		☐
7	Casual blazer		☐
8	Sweater or cardigan		☐
9	Dress pants		☐
10	Khaki or chinos		☐
11	**Basic Accessories**	**Details: colour, prints, shape, brand, size**	✔
12	Leather belt; one colour		☐
13	Leather city shoes		☐
14	Tie		☐
15	Three neutral socks		☐
16	Two accent socks		☐
17	**Basic Seasonal Wear**	**Details: colour, prints, shape, brand, size**	✔
18	Coat	Longer than your longest jacket	☐
19	Boots		☐
20	Scarf, gloves and hat		☐
	Multi-purpose bag		☐
	Umbrella		☐

It all starts with a full-length mirror.

10-10 WARDROBE GUIDELINES – MAN

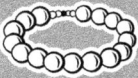

When buying items of clothing, prefer:

- Quality over quantity, especially for your basic suit
- Neutral colours over colourful prints
- Versatile over unique match pieces
- Classic over trendy
- All-season wear over seasonal wear

MEN'S FASHION BASICS

- Two fingers should slip between your neck and collar.

- Sleeves are 5 inches (12 centimeters) from the thumb, at the wrist bone.

- Shirtsleeves or cuffs are ¼ inch (0.6 centimeters) to ½ inch (0.3 centimeters) from the end of the jacket's sleeve.

- The tie tip falls one-quarter inch (0.6 centimeters) below your belt.

- The bottom button of your suit is always undone.

- Trousers are hemmed at the top of the shoe with a front crease.

- Shoes match the occasion. Belts generally match shoes. Socks match pants or offer a whimsical complementary touch. Personally, I always love the discreet surprise of argyle or red socks when a man crosses his legs.

Excerpt from **ETIQUETTE: CONFIDENCE & CREDIBILITY**

10-10 WARDROBE GUIDELINES – MAN

MY PERSONAL PROFESSIONAL WARDROBE SHOPPING INFORMATION ....

My body shape _____

My wardrobe colours _____

My style _____

My jacket size _____

My pants size _____

My shirt size _____

My shoe size _____

My belt size _____

With the previous ten basic workwear items, you can build ten outfits for all of the professional activities that you may encounter over the course of two weeks.

10-10 WARDROBE CHECKLIST – WOMAN

#	Basic Workwear	Details: colour, prints, shape, brand, size	✔
1	Suit blazer		☐
2	Suit pants		☐
3	Suit skirt		☐
4	White collar blouse		☐
5	Solid top		☐
6	Print top		☐
7	Casual blazer		☐
8	Sweater or cardigan		☐
9	Other pants or skirt		☐
10	Basic dress		☐
11	**Basic Accessories**	**Details: colour, prints, shape, brand, size**	✔
12	Basic make-up		☐
13	Multi-purpose bag		☐
14	Pumps		☐
15	Lower heel shoes		☐
16	Natural stockings		☐
17	Accent socks		☐
18	Pearls		☐
19	Diamond studs		☐
20	Belt		☐
21	Scarf with print		☐
22	**Basic Seasonal Wear**	**Details: colour, prints, shape, brand, size**	✔
23	Coat	Longer than your longest jacket	☐
24	Boots		☐
25	Scarf, gloves and hat		☐
	Multi-purpose bag		☐
	Umbrella		☐

It all starts with a full-length mirror.

Excerpt from ***ETIQUETTE: CONFIDENCE & CREDIBILITY***

10-10 WARDROBE GUIDELINES – WOMAN

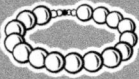

When buying items of clothing, prefer:
- Quality over quantity, especially for your basic suit
- Neutral colours over colourful prints
- Versatile over unique match pieces
- Classic over trendy
- All-season wear over seasonal wear

WOMEN'S FASHION BASICS

- Respect Hand–High and Hand–Low hem and cleavage guidelines. Hand–High = the appropriate hemline height: while sitting, place your hand above your knee, with your pinkie at the top of your knee. Let your relaxed hand lay flat on your thigh. Where your thumb rests, is the shortest your skirt or dress should rise for an appropriate professional hemline. Hand–Low = appropriate cleavage depth: place your hand at the base of your neck, with your thumb in the little hole between your top ribs. Let your relaxed hand fall. Where your pinkie drops is the depth of appropriate professional cleavage.

- Your underwear should of course be comfortable, but always remain a secret.

- Shoes match the occasion.

- Acceptable shoe heel height is what you can professionally walk on. If you are not comfortable, steady or too self-conscious, people will look at your walk instead of focusing on your performance.

- Stockings and panty hose match your natural skin tone and are not darker or lighter.

- Twelve is the maximum number of accessories you should wear at a time. Do not forget to count nail polish, eyeglasses, coloured stockings or buttons as part of your accessories.

- Carry your items in one quality multi-purpose bag along with your purse.

Excerpt from ***ETIQUETTE: CONFIDENCE & CREDIBILITY***

10-10 WARDROBE GUIDELINES – WOMAN

MY PERSONAL PROFESSIONAL WARDROBE SHOPPING INFORMATION ....

My body shape _____

My wardrobe colours _____

My style _____

My jacket size _____

My pants size _____

My blouse size _____

My dress size _____

My shoe size _____

With the previous ten basic workwear Items, you can build ten outfits for all of the professional activities that you may encounter over the course of two weeks.

Excerpt from ***ETIQUETTE: CONFIDENCE & CREDIBILITY***

The numbers below refer to the numbers of your basic work wear items in your wardrobe checklist. Experiment with your 10–10 Professional Wardrobe by filling out the above empty boxes to create unique, once in a two-week cycle ensembles based on your checklist.

Week 1	Monday	Tuesday	Wednesday	Thursday	Friday
Professional Activity	Presenting to Client			Cocktail Networking	
Man	1 + 2 + 4			1 + 5 + 9	
Woman	1 + 3 + 6			1 + 10	
Week 2	Monday	Tuesday	Wednesday	Thursday	Friday
Professional Activity			Team Meeting		Casual Friday
Man			3 + 8 + 9		6 + 10
Woman			2 + 5 + 7		5 + 8 + 9

On Sunday evening, prepare your week's work-wear ensembles on individual hangers and include their accompanying accessories.

–Time saving tip from an IT Business Development client following her *Dress for Success* private coaching session.

| SOLUTIONS TO STICKY WARDROBE MALFUNCTIONS

Pop! Oooh noooo...What?

Nobody can see anything. You have not missed a beat. You recognize all too well that sinking feeling. It is not a regular sensation but a very familiar one. Your button popped. You came undone. Your pants, your shirt, your blouse or your bra feel a little looser, freer. This is not a good thing.

You are in the middle of a sales pitch to a client. On the outside, you try your best to keep calm. You carry on. On the inside, your mind is going one hundred miles an hour doing a complete inventory of your pockets, your bag, your desk if you are at the office, maybe even your car. You may even have started to scout the conference room in search of a forgotten sewing kit.

Why am I introducing this scenario? To get you prepared. As a contemporary employee, expect the worst, and be prepared for the best.

Wardrobe malfunctions do not just happen to Hollywood stars. They can happen to any one of us, at any moment. Actually, they usually happen at the most inopportune time—not necessarily in front of the cameras, but probably in front of your boss or your client. Yes, believe me. I can personally attest to a couple of these embarrassing moments. Yikes! How I wish I could permanently delete them.

In anticipation of your next 911–dress distress, here is a list of Sticky Wardrobe Malfunction Solutions.

STICKY WARDROBE MALFUNCTION SOLUTIONS

Bad hair day

A little dab will do you. Run, water mixed with a little bit of gel, or a dab of lotion through your hair, and brush or comb. Do not forget the back of your head. Ladies, paper clips can come to the rescue. Use them to create an up do.

Bloating

Maybe you had a little too much for lunch. Undo your button, thread an elastic band through the buttonhole and loop it around the button. Now that feels better.

Boss unexpectedly calls to take you out to lunch

Keep an extra jacket or blazer and tie, on a hanger behind your door. Also, keep a shoe buffer at work. Rub a bit of lotion; any kind will do, as a substitute.

Broken zipper

When a tooth is missing near the bottom, zip up the zipper above the damage. Make several stitches above the missing tooth, to make a new stop for the slider. Use a safety pin to replace a missing pull tab.

> What does the YKK, found on most zippers, mean?
> YKK makes zippers and other fastening products.
> Yoshida Kōgyō Kabushiki Kaisha founded the company
> in 1934 in Tokyo.

Broken shoelace

Tie the ends together and make sure the knot is under the eyelet. Alternatively, coat the ends in glue and let them dry before putting it back on. Keep an extra pair of shoelaces.

Chipped nail

You have options: file it down, cut the tip of your nail, reapply polish or add a bandage to cover it up. Chipped nails are a pet peeve of mine. I always carry my latest nail polish bottle with me, just in case.

---

[17] http://germguy.wordpress.com/author/jtetro

STICKY WARDROBE MALFUNCTION SOLUTIONS

Drippy nose and/or watery eyes

Inhale one sniff per nostril of a medicinal inhaler stick, to relieve congestion or hay fever symptoms. This is especially effective before a presentation. In my experience, I am clear and dry for up to two hours. This sticky situation solution is a courtesy of the Germ Guy Jason Tetro[17]. Thanks Jason.

Deodorant stains

Gently rub baby wipes on the stain. Never use a wet paper towel! It will worsen your stain and will leave fluff on your garment. Rubbing fabric against fabric also works.

Exposed metal heel

Remove the pink eraser from the end of your classic HB pencil. If necessary, cut it to the appropriate height. Glue it to the end of your exposed metal heel. You are now good to go, safely.

Falling button

Never leave home without a pre-threaded needle or a safety pin. They, along with double-sided tape will re-attach your button.

Forgotten collar stays

Steady your collar tips back in shape by inserting paper clips in lieu of stays or sticks.

Fuzzy sweater, jacket, blazer or coat and lint

To catch the lint, use tape, placed inside out on the back of a brush or even your stapler.

Hem that is coming undone

Attach the hem by using grooming tape, double-sided tape, a pre-threaded needle or even a stapler.

Popped bra strap

Attach it with a safety pin, a paper clip or sew it with a pre-threaded needle.

Peek-a-boo cleavage

Use double-sided tape to secure opening shirts or blouses.

Run in hose

An oldie but goodie, paint clear nail polish on the run. It will stop it from stretching.

Excerpt from *ETIQUETTE: CONFIDENCE & CREDIBILITY*

STICKY WARDROBE MALFUNCTION SOLUTIONS

Scuffed up shoes or bag
Fill it in with the same colour permanent marker. Use any oil to buff it back to shine.

Sore feet
Wear insoles and shoe pads. Keep a pair of flats at work to change when needed.

Stain(s)
A portable stick stain remover is essential. Wet towelettes are best for white fabrics. Hairspray also works, especially on leather by dabbing it with white tissue paper.

Static
Rub a sheet of fabric softener or a metal hanger on your garment. This tip is graciously offered by a personal stylist colleague, Lyne Ratté[18]. Merci Lyne.

Sweaty armpits or feet
Add a tiny bit of baby powder in the toes of your shoes and in the armpits of your shirt.

Torn clothing
Place tape (duct tape works best) on the inside of the tear.

Wet socks
Wet feet can be debilitating. Keep an extra pair of socks.

Wrinkled clothes
Spray your item with wrinkle remover. At home, tumble your garment in a medium setting dryer with a damp facecloth and a sheet of softener, for 10 minutes. You can also hang your garment in the bathroom while you shower.

Wrinkled scarves
Install a towel rack behind your closet or bedroom door. Place your scarves over the rod. They will never have fold lines.

Zipper that is stuck
Color it with your pencil. The lead will lubricate it so that you can zip it back up.

---

[18] http://www.lyneratte.com/

Excerpt from *ETIQUETTE: CONFIDENCE & CREDIBILITY*

| KEEP AN EMERGENCY KIT AT THE OFFICE

From splitting headaches to slipping zippers, an office emergency kit will keep you fresh and confident in the face of the most unexpected wardrobe malfunctions during the most important business activities.

From the previous Sticky Wardrobe Malfunction Solutions, you may have learned a few tricks while mentally starting to build your own work survival essentials.

Here is a list of mishap must haves. Add your favourites at the bottom and please let me know what they are at julie@etiquettejulie.com and I will share them with others.

Assemble your office emergency kit into an empty shoebox, a crafty pouch or a plastic freezer bag. Print and place the Dress Distress Cheat sheets in it. Being as prepared as a scout, is a good thing.

Adhesive bandages		Medicated inhaler stick	
Baby-wipe towelettes		Medicine for your aches and pains	
Blazer or jacket		Mints not gum*	
Elastic bands		Needles; pre-threaded ones are ideal	
Clear nail polish		Paper clip	
Deodorant		Permanent marker	
Double-sided tape		Pencil with top eraser	
Elastic bands		Safety pins	
Emery board		Shoe buffer	
Earring backs		Stain remover pen	
Extra laces and socks for men		Static guard spray	
Extra hose and socks for women		Tape	
Feet cushions		Tie	
Flat shoes in a neutral colour		Toiletries in sample sizes	
Hair comb or brush		White shirt	
Hairspray		Wrinkle free spray	
Hand sanitizer			
Headache relief			
Make-up basics			
Manicure clippers that include a file			

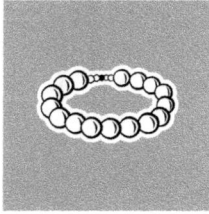

> In my professional opinion, gum should be a solitary activity. When you chew it, it has a life of its own. You relax, forget you have it and the next thing you know, you are making funny sounds or showing your fillings. Granted, gum also has the added value of keeping you focused on tasks and may also increase your retention. So keep it for private moments.

Picture this. You bend to plug in your laptop. The outlet is just a little further away. You stretch a little more. You are almost there. S–tttt–retch a little bit more…All of a sudden you stop. Your jacket is caught. You hear a definitely identifiable sound. Ohhh, you feel a little looser…Oh no…Your heart races. You did not see it. The popping screw was hidden behind the bracket. Your cheeks flush. What can you do?

If you are prepared with a complete change of clothes, you will soon find relief in your backup attire. Within minutes of politely excusing yourself to the washroom, you will return fresh, confident and credible. How do I know? It happened to me. Yup! Take my word for it—bring the extra outfit.

| DECODE THE DRESS CODES

By his clothing choices, the Canadian world-re-nowned singer, writer and producer, Justin Bieber, sent two very different messages about meeting the American and the Canadian, Heads of State.

In Canada, in his homeland, the pop icon wore overalls and a ball cap to receive Queen Elizabeth II's Diamond Jubilee Medal from Prime Minister Stephen Harper.

On the opposite end of the spectrum of dress codes, when invited to sing *Hark! The Herald Angels Sing* at Washington's National Building Museum for the annual Christmas in Washington event, the teen sensation wore a chic contemporary and youthful tuxedo.

I have not had the privilege of speaking with Mr. Bieber or one of his public relations staff members, so I do not know what prompted him to wear such extreme attires for similar meetings with two world leaders.

Just by looking at the photos that circulated on the internet, I, and many of Bieber's most loyal fans, thought that he paid more respect to American President Barack Obama than his own Canadian head of state. What do you think?

Regardless of what you and I think, about these two occasions, Justin broadcasted two different messages, just with his clothing.

As you walk down the hall, your boss calls out your name. You stop in your tracks, turn around and walk into her office. You look in as she lifts her head from her notebook. She waves at you and invites you in. From across her desk, she hands you a fancy square envelope with your name "and guest" written in beautiful calligraphic letters. "This is for you. Open it." You do as she asks and open it. It is an exclusive invitation to the annual sales banquet. "You made the top five!" she cheers. She informs you that you are on the short list to receive the top sales person of the year award. The name of the top performer is traditionally announced during the gala reception. Wow, you are thrilled! You look at her and beam.

You glance over the invitation as she fills you in on the details for the evening. Your heart starts to race and your smile quickly turns to terror as you notice Black Tie Required in the bottom right corner of the invitation. What does black tie mean? Will your black suit, white shirt and black tie work? Will your partner need to buy a gown?

Relax. You are not alone. Dress codes can send many professionals into a spiral of questions. Typically, the rarer the event, the more formal the dress code will be. The more formal the event; the darker your suit should be.

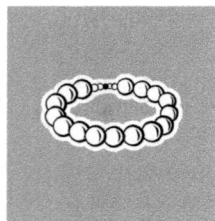

Dress codes are based on:

- The occasion
- The circumstances
- The venue
- The time of day

By informing guests of the dress code, a host is setting you up for success, while ensuring that the level of formality that he/she has chosen for the event will be respected. Whatever the dress code is, you are expected to show up in it.

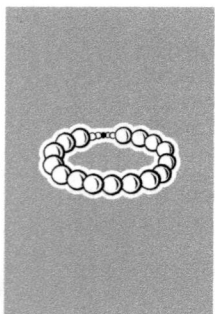

If for whatever reason—too costly, you do not feel like it or your attire is at the cleaner's, you cannot dress according to the requested dress code, promptly send your regrets. Simply stated, do not go. Showing up in less than expected wear is disrespectful. I doubt that any host would ask you to turn around and go change but not dressing up to par is inappropriate. You do not need that kind of negative attention being brought to yourself. Keep in line with the S.E.S. philosophy and you will be able to tackle any invitation.

DRESS CODES DECODED

Code Occasion	Man	Woman
Casual • Informal gathering with friends/family members • Invitation comes by telephone or email	• Remove all hats indoors	• Fashion hats may be worn before 6:00 p.m.
	• General weekend wear • Avoid t-shirts with disrespectful logos or sayings • Resist the urge to overdress	
Business Casual • At the office or after office hours • Usually addressed in company dress code policy	• Closed shoes and socks	• No bare shoulders
	• No to the 4 Bs; Beach wear, Bar wear, Boudoir wear or Barbell (gym) wear, including white athletic socks and running shoes • No sunglasses • No flip flops: they are noisy, could be smelly and seeing the big boss' big toe or the little boss' little toe, is way too much information • Dressy jeans when accepted	
Dressy Casual • Sportswear • Gatherings for colleagues/friends/family members	• Sport jacket or blazer • Dress pants • Open necked shirt • Turtleneck • Optional tie or ascot	• Dress • Dressy skirt and top • Dressy pants suit
Business Formal • Cocktail or reception	• Suit • Dress shirt • Tie • Leather shoes	• Suit • Blouse or shirt • Work dress • Close toe pump
Semi Formal • Cocktail or reception • Invitation is for before 6:00 p.m.	• Dark suit • Vest optional • Tie or bow tie • Cufflinks optional • Formal shoes	• Cocktail dress • Dressy separates or suit • Long skirt and dressy top • Sandals or dressy pumps

Excerpt from *ETIQUETTE: CONFIDENCE & CREDIBILITY*

DRESS CODES DECODED

Code Occasion	Man	Woman
Formal Black Tie • Generally an evening event; a ball, the opera or receptions	• Black or midnight blue tuxedo • White dress shirt • Silk bow tie • Waist coat or cummerbund • Cufflinks • Black patent leather shoes	• Floor length gown • Tea length dress (to the calf) • Cocktail dress • Evening shoes • Gloves are optional; if worn they are removed once at the table to eat and drink
Formal White Tie • The most formal of civilian dress codes	• Evening tail coat • Pants with satin braid • Stiff front white shirt • White vest • White bow tie • Black patent leather shoes and black socks • White or gray gloves optional	• Long evening gown • Gloves are optional

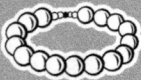

Men and women may rent their black or white tie formal wear. This will reduce the cost per occasion. Instead of relegating sequins and tuxedos to the back of closets to collect dust, it also encourages recycling.

When you receive an after 6:00 p.m. invitation that does not indicate a dress code, a lounge suit for men and an afternoon dress for women are recommended.

When in doubt about the dress code, find out. It is always acceptable to call your host, the organizers or the coordinator to find out how to dress.

Cocktail is not a dress code. Cocktail on an invitation refers to what will be served at that time of the day. Cocktail was 1st defined in 1806 as stimulating liquor. Cocktail therefore is exclusively limited to the drink that you may have. People wrongly use it to define a dress code or even pre-meal appetizers.

Excerpt from ***ETIQUETTE: CONFIDENCE & CREDIBILITY***

| FEEL THE CLOTHING CONNECTION

Clothing has symbolism. Clothing empowers. Clothing puts you into character for your role in the business world. Clothing affects your body and your brain.

> A Kellogg School of Management at Northwestern University study confirmed that not only do we think with our brain; we also think with our bodies.
>
> Undergraduate subjects who wore white lab coats and were told they belonged to doctors displayed better attention than their counterparts who were told that their white lab coats belonged to painters.
>
> Both groups had to identify differences in similar side-by-side pictures.
>
> –*Enclothed Cognition*; Journal of Experimental Social Psychology

You are what you wear. The choice is yours. Who and what do you want to be?

If you are seeking a promotion, make your apparel selection similar to that of your direct superiors. You want to look like you are part of their team so take your cues from the ones above you.

Be careful not to clone or to emulate too high up on the pecking order of your organization. This will have an adverse effect on your promotion seeking attempts.

SUMMARY

- Recognize your body's shape and dress to accent or minimize your body parts.
- Remember that clothing guides people's glances.
- Use colors to influence your mood and to suit the occasion or organization.
- Accessorize to enhance your outfit without distracting.
- Ladies, go get fitted for the proper bra.
- Seasonally build a 10-10 wardrobe.
- Keep an emergency kit at the office.
- Respect dress codes.

The modern day accessory of today's contemporary employee is the cell phone. Although a necessity for most of us, it should not always be visible. Now that we have covered how to dress for professional success, let's take a look at cell phone etiquette and how you can communicate correctly with all forms of contemporary technology.

COMMUNICATE CORRECTLY WITH TECHNOLOGY

I fear that the day that technology will surpass our human interaction, the world will have a generation of idiots.

–Albert Einstein

Communication in itself is simple. It only contains three elements: the sender, the receiver and the message. Successful communication, no matter what channel you use, is only achieved when the intentions of your message are those received by the other party.

Do you remember playing the telephone game? You probably played it in elementary school when your substitute teacher used this quiet activity to calm your class.

You whispered a short sentence to your neighbour. She repeated it to the next student and so on, until it came full circle back to you. The last one of your classmates to receive the message said it aloud. The teacher then called on you to state your original sentence. The class would then hysterically laugh as "Cantaloupes are good for you in the evening" became "Fruit loops are great in the morning!" How could that be? Maybe a car alarm went off, and Gigi misunderstood a word. Maybe Frances did not understand a word and replaced it with another. Maybe Alexander was laughing right through his turn and so Christopher made up a completely new sentence.

Beyond the telephone, communication technologies have evolved. Today's professionals have many channels of communication at their disposal, to send their message.

How many communication channels do you use at work? "Let me count the ways", you answer, as you count with your fingers, "Email, texting, tweeting… and oh yes…the office telephone…I guess it doesn't really count. I only used it on my first day at work to record my outgoing message." You bring your index finger to your chin, and continue: "There is also videoconferencing.

Does Facebook count too?" you ask, as you point your first digit up in the air.

In today's technological world, you can communicate in person with your cubicle neighbour; exchange emails with your entire east coast team or watch your CEO share the year's objectives on a worldwide videoconference.

Each communication channel has its purpose. Consider the advantages and disadvantages of each channel. Based on the receiver of your message, choose the most appropriate channel for your message. By choosing wisely you will achieve successful communication more quickly and ultimately you will be more productive.

COMMUNICATION ACTIVITIES ASSESSMENT

Let us look at how you communicate.

1. Review the list of communication channels below and input missing channels, if any, to reflect your business communications.

2. Place a check mark next to all of the communication channels that you use at work.

3. Input the percentage each channel represents when considering your overall communications. If you are not sure about the numbers, track your communications for one week and then input them into the table.

4. List the purposes and the reasons for using each of the communication channels.

5. Add its advantages and disadvantages.

Communication Chanel	✔	%	Communication Purposes	Advantages	Disadvantages
Cell Phone					
Email					
In Person					
Letter					
Social Network					
Telephone					
Texting					
Video Conference					

You now have a clear picture of your communication activities.

You probably can conclude that the more personal your message is, the more interactive you want the communication to be. In the same fashion, the less personal the message is, the less important is the need for a method that provides an opportunity for feedback.

Excerpt from *ETIQUETTE: CONFIDENCE & CREDIBILITY*

In Guideline 2—*TAKE CONTROL OF YOUR FIRST IMPRESSIONS*, you learned that the most effective way of communicating is in person. The other channels lack the value of these collective clues: the visual, the verbal and the vocal clues, or a combination of these.

In your career, you communicate to ask, inform, educate, obtain feedback, influence and thank. Depending on your communication purpose, your choice of medium will greatly influence the effectiveness of your message. Effective communication is more than just fitting the technology to your message's intentions. Effective communication also needs to be adapted to its recipient.

Picture this. You and your boss Marty, are expected Monday at 9:00 a.m. at a prospective client's office to present your proposal. Marty gets there early. From his cell, he calls his secretary Sue, to review the upcoming week's activities.

It is 8:50 a.m. and you are running late. You send a text to your boss to let him know that you are running 20 minutes behind.

He tells his assistant that his battery is dying and will catch up with her when he gets to the office. To allow the battery to recharge, he plugs his telephone in his car. He then steps outside to stretch his legs. He looks at his watch; it is 8:55 a.m.

You have still not arrived. He decides to go in to meet with your client.

You get there at 9:10 a.m. and join the meeting, already in progress. An hour later, after a stellar presentation and a brief Q & A, all shake hands. You did it! They signed the deal. You exit and high five your boss.

When you reach the sidewalk, he asks you why you were late. "Did you not get my text?" "No. I had to recharge my telephone. It kept on beeping while I was on the phone with Sue." In reality, the beeps were signalling your incoming text message but he did not know it. Your superior is 58 years old and has never texted before. He did not know his telephone could receive text messages much less that they would be announced with a beep.

Yes, this is an extreme example, but the point is that in order to have successful communication you must make sure the communication channel is appropriate for your message as well as its receiver.

Besides generational diversity, today's workplace also includes: gender, cultural, physical, geographical, educational and technological differences that must be considered when communicating.

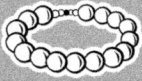

Even though surveys confirm that our DNA is 99.9 percent the same, people are different. Our DNA counts some three billion elements. At 0.01 percent, our differences add up to three million possibilities! These differences account for how we look and how we behave.

Successful communication adapts to those differences. I am not saying to be a chameleon, but I recommend that you fit your message to its recipient.

Choose a communication method that will ensure that the other party understands your message as you intended it.

| TELEPHONE

As demonstrated with your communication table, the telephone may not be the dominant means of communication in your daily routine, but it certainly is crucial for the maintenance of your business relationships.

The way that you answer a call or the way you introduce yourself when you place a call, will contribute to your colleagues' and clients' perceptions of you.

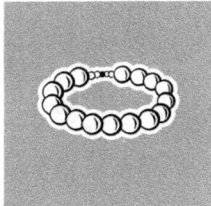

Keep all telephone call notes in a notebook. My favourite is a nine inches by six inches spiral notebook. I carry it everywhere. In it I input, not only the details of my telephone calls but I also include those of all of my meetings; in person, on the telephone or videoconferencing. The advantage of spiral bound is that you can remove a sheet without destroying the entire book.

- When a disconnection occurs, it is the caller's responsibility to call back. This etiquette rule applies to cell phone, landline, Skype, face time or any other outbound calling media.

- If there is a bad connection, it is always appropriate to ask the other party to hang up, so you can call back for a better connection.

- If you have caller identification, do not answer the telephone by stating the caller's name. It is creepy, especially if it is someone that you have only met a couple of times.

As an HR manager, I was constantly in search of the best talent in retail. I have recruited and selected from hundreds of resumes. Once I had my list of candidates, I would dial them up for a preliminary interview. There is a lot that you can find out from a simple impromptu call and someone's voicemail message. If a prospective employer was calling, right now, would you be ready?

Listen to your own voicemail. Is there anything that you can improve on?

What about your general phone manners? Find out in this next activity.

TELEPHONE ETIQUETTE SELF-EVALUATION

Let us evaluate your current telephone manners at the office. Go through the list below and rate yourself by assigning 1 to 5 points for each of the following guidelines:

5 = Always **4** = Almost always **3** = Regularly **2** = Sometimes **1** = Never

	Telephone Etiquette Guidelines	Points
1	I prepare notes, questions and have all the necessary documents for my call.	
2	I input call notes legibly in a spiral bound notebook to be able to refer back to them.	
3	If I am working on a priority, I let my voicemail answer the call.	
4	I answer the telephone with a smile in my voice. I state my name and department, if applicable. For a bilingual call answer, keep it simple. For example, "Bonjour, this is Julie."	
5	I give all of my attention to the caller: no typing, no reading emails, no eating, no filing folders, no nail clipping, no gum chewing or clicking of my pen.	
6	I inform callers when I use speakerphone.	
7	When others are present on the call with me, I make the necessary introductions.	
8	When placing a caller on hold, I first ask permission, give the reason for the hold, the expected delay, and regularly give a progress update, if it exceeds 2 minutes.	
9	When transferring a call, I give the other person's name, their extension and stay on the line until they pick up or offer to take a message.	
10	I respect the other party's time by: ending telephone meetings on time or suggesting another call meeting time. When returning calls, I avoid telephone tag by stating ideal times to reach me or give the time and day that I will call back.	

Excerpt from ***ETIQUETTE: CONFIDENCE & CREDIBILITY***

TELEPHONE ETIQUETTE SELF-EVALUATION

	Telephone Etiquette Guidelines	Points
11	When I place a call, I start by stating my first and last name with the purpose for my call.	
12	I summarize all calls in a positive way by stating next steps. I make sure that I have those written down legibly to be able to refer to them.	
13	My voicemail greeting is brief, up to date and gives the number for a live person or my email address. Note: If your message must be bilingual, alternate languages without duplicating the information.	
14	When leaving a message, I slowly state my name and telephone number at the start and at the end.	
15	I use a headset to minimize ambient sounds and to accentuate the sound of my voice.	
	TOTAL	

55 and less—Revise the above guidelines and apply them daily.

56 to 66—You know what to do, you are just missing consistency.

67 and more—Wow! You are a telephone service professional!

_____

_____

_____

_____

_____

_____

_____

| MOBILE TELEPHONE

You panic when you do not touch it, feel it or see it. You never leave home without it. You never get into your car without first connecting it to your headset. You carry it in your pocket, your purse, or on your hip. You leave it on the counter, the table or your desk. Do you also take it to the bathroom?

> Three-quarters of Americans use, including talk, on their mobile telephones while they are in the bathroom.
>
> 63 percent of respondents have answered a call and 41 percent have initiated a call.
>
> 20 percent of men and 13 percent of women have participated in work-related calls.
>
> –2012 IT in the Toilet study of 1000 Americans by 11mark

Remember this: whether you text, talk, tweet or tag, your alone time is no longer private. Whatever happens behind closed stalls does not always stay behind closed stalls.

You know of the advantages of smart telephones and recognize the freedom that they give you to stay connected, get the information, immortalize a moment, or to reach out in the case of an emergency.

You also probably have at least three stories of smart phone abuse and know of at least one person who is addicted to his/her mobile device and needs to separate him/herself from the phone. If you are a Y-Gen (generation of persons born between the end of the 1970s and 2000), you may even be immune to cell phone etiquette faux pas.

For some users, there may be a fine line between telephone use and abuse. Let us review responsible smart telephone guidelines. Used in moderation, a smart phone is an intelligent way of conducting business.

SOUND AND WARDROBE CHECKS, TEST; ONE, TWO ...

Your ring tone and telephone cover contribute as much to your brand as you do. Choose them wisely.

LOCATION, LOCATION, LOCATION

When alone in public, in places such as a library, a restaurant or while on public transportation, use texting instead of talking to communicate.

YOU ARE THE BOSS OF YOUR TELEPHONE

Do not let your telephone interrupt your life. Because it is ringing does not mean that you have to answer it. Look and listen around you. Who could you be disturbing? What could your caller be hearing? Choose whether it is appropriate to take the call or if it would be best to let your voicemail do its job. You decide, if you should answer, or not.

FACETIME ALWAYS HAS PRECEDENCE OVER SCREEN TIME

When you are in the presence of others; meeting a client, attending a networking event or participating in a business meeting; your mobile device should be in polite silent mode.

A vibrating telephone is disturbing especially if it is doing the snake on the conference table.

Of course, there are exceptions, as when you are waiting for information that will contribute to the meeting or when you are the lifeline to a loved one. In those instances, inform your counterpart at the onset of your meeting.

When your call comes, politely excuse yourself. Inform the caller that you are with someone, and that you are moving to a location where you can converse.

PLEASE, THEN CHEESE

Before taking a photo of someone or recording a presentation, always ask permission. Because you have the technology, it does not mean that you have the right to use it.

KEEP IT PG 13, BIG BROTHER IS LISTENING

Watch your language and never discuss business matters or personal matters when in public. You could be breaching a confidentiality agreement or making others feel uncomfortable.

> Use your cell phone as you would a public telephone; knowing that someone is listening and waiting.

| TEXT MESSAGES

> "Merry Christmas" these two words made up the very first text. It is on December 3rd, 1992 that British engineer Neil Papworth, of the U.K.'s Sema Group, sent his original seasonal wish on the Vodafone network. The message traveled from his computer to his colleague's telephone.

Although it is two decades old, texting is the new it thing, for keeping in touch.

Convenient and fast, texting can touch someone's life immediately and forever. Think of 9/11 or Tiger Woods' famous sext messages. Texts affect lives.

Touch the keys, press send and instantly; through a vibration, your message touches someone's hip and maybe someone's heart. Touched, they have your attention. Is your message an interaction or an interruption?

When invited to give a business etiquette workshop, managers now request that I include a texting module. The dos and don'ts of this casual mode of communication can tarnish a company's or an employee's reputation quickly and permanently.

Here are 20 business textiquette guidelines to keep your interactions positive and interruption free.

INQUIRE ABOUT THE OTHER'S TEXTING CAPACITY ...

When involved in a new business relationship, validate communication expectations, including their ability to receive attachments and photos.

INTRODUCE YOURSELF ....

With a new contact or when you are the first to initiate a texting conversation, start the conversation by identifying yourself.

IN THE COMPANY OF OTHERS, INFORM OF AN IMPORTANT INCOMING TEXT ....

For example, if your teenager is on a trip to Europe, and you are expecting a "Touchdown. Safely arrived" text, inform your colleague at the beginning of the meeting. Once received, turn your mobile device to OFF.

BE BRIEF AND PRECISE

Generally, a text is one or two sentences. Keep in mind; telephone screen sizes are not universal. What fits on your screen may necessitate scrolling on another telephone. Some texting packages are based on the number of characters. If your text extends past a couple of sentences, pick up the telephone or send an email.

PROOFREAD YOUR MESSAGES

An intended text to your boss: "Getting a cook book" for your totally foodie client's birthday could read: "Getting a coke book". Consider disabling your telephone's autocorrect options. I have.

GIVE THE BENEFIT OF TIME

Patience. Because you have texted and maybe touched someone does not mean that the other person is in a position or location to reply immediately.

RESPECT TEXTING TIME ZONES

Texting hours mirror extended business hours, such as 7 a.m. to 7 p.m.; keep in mind that our world currently has 24 standard time zones.

WHEN RUNNING LATE, INCLUDE EXPECTED TIME OF ARRIVAL (ETA)

"Running late. ETA 12:15 p.m." This practice avoids wasting more time on subsequent texts. The expected time of arrival also gives the other person the opportunity to occupy their newly found time.

RARELY MASS SEND

As with email, create groups. For example, would you want all of your contacts, including your Montreal client, to receive "GO SENS GO. HABS SU_ _" as you watch the game.

LIMIT STALL TEXTING

I caught you! You send text messages while in the washroom, don't you?

> 69% of the one thousand surveyed admitted to keeping their digits busy while sitting on the throne.
>
> –2012 IT in the Toilet study of 1000 Americans by 11mark

In the privacy of the toilet walls, it is easy to get lost in time and to forget about the client who is waiting alone at the table or the others in line waiting for their turn.

SEND THANK YOU TEXTS

It is the new way of giving a pat on the back. Text and touch someone's ego with virtual high fives!

LET THE OTHER KNOW WHEN IT IS A WRONG NUMBER

Wrong number telephone etiquette also applies to texting. Simply text "Sorry, wrong number."

END THE CONVERSATION

It does not have to be lengthy, a simple THX (thanks) or TTYL (talk to you later) are acceptable and will not keep the other person waiting for more.

> Are you wondering what all the cool persons are texting? Check out this list of acronyms and shorthand messages:
> http://www.netlingo.com/acronyms.php

DO NOT DRIVE AND TEXT

> Close to one in five Canadians admitted to texting while driving.
>
> –2012 *Kanetix Driving Habits in Canada*

The text you send while driving could touch death: yours, that of one of your passengers or other drivers. Your employer and especially your loved ones want you to pledge to never text and drive. Your life depends on it. Do it. Pledge not to text and drive. Thank you.

> If your colleague is texting and driving while you are traveling together, say something like "I know that you are busy, so I propose that I drive. This way you can continue your work and I promise to take good care of your car."

DO NOT SEND SAD, BAD, PRIVATE, EMBARRASSING OR CONFIDENTIAL NEWS

If you find it difficult to share the news or the information in person, do not hide behind a text. Breathe in. Find your courage for an in person meeting. Do you need more guidance? Read my *Sticky Situations* blog Bad News Guide—What to Do and Say[19].

Although you may think that your texting conversation is one-on-one, think again. Come back to reality! With a couple of taps, your message can go viral.

As you would not break up a romantic relationship by texting, do not end a business relationship with a text.

DO NOT REPLY WITH SARCASTIC OR RUDE REMARKS

A text can quickly escalate from funny and witty to hurtful and unprofessional.

NO TEXTING WHILE WALKING

Texting while walking can be plain dangerous, not to mention embarrassing. Gentlemen, imagine showing up at a meeting with a client while having spilled coffee on your white shirt. Ladies, imagine showing up at the office with your left heel missing.

NO TEXTING WHILE DRINKING

Yes, I know that you know. It is worth repeating. Your vocabulary may be smoother or slicker after your first drink but come the morning after, you may wish that you could have touched up or tossed out your text, before touching send. Do not text while drinking.

DO NOT TEXT INVITATIONS

An email, an electronic invitation or a telephone call is a better option for business invitations. Changing meeting plans should also be done by telephone, especially for last minute changes.

DO NOT SEND MORE THAN ONE ATTACHMENT OR LINK PER TEXT

If you need to send many attachments or links, send an email.

---

[19] http://www.etiquettejulie.com/?q=story/what-do-and-say

In conclusion, text and touch thoughtfully. When typing on your telephone's keys and before touching send, ask yourself "Could this text be a rude interruption or, is it a convenient communication?"

TTFN (Ta Ta For Now).

| EMAILS

> Ray Tomlinson, an American computer engineer, graduate of the Rensselaer Polytechnic Institute, sent the first email in late 1971.
>
> He is also credited with the use of the @ symbol to separate names from domains.

Email benefits include global communication with out of office clients and colleagues, reduced paper consumption and most of all, the speedy exchange of information. This last feature has also landed many employees in sticky situations.

Your company probably has provided you with their set of electronic guidelines, including how to protect confidential documents, how to archive and destroy files. Respect them. When in doubt, find out.

Although you do not have a physical person in front of you when you communicate with electronic correspondence, your message is still destined to a human being. Contrary to when you are having a live conversation in private, your email may quickly become public. The words you type are permanent. They may be forwarded, printed and shared.

To ensure that your emails contribute to your professional image, increase your productivity and protect you from liable situations, consider the following guidelines before pressing the SEND button.

Emailing by the numbers

- Average number of emails sent and received per user per day: 110
- Average number of emails received: 74
- Average number of legitimate emails (not including spam): 61
- Average number of emails sent: 36

  –Email Statistics Report, 2010; The Radicati Group, Inc.

FROM

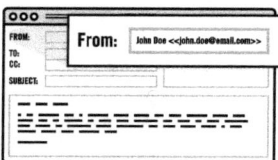

Make sure that your name is properly displayed with proper capitalization.

If you are job seeking, use your real name in your email address. Doctorlove@hotmail.com only works if you are a marriage counsellor.

You may also wish to add the name of your company. For example, *Julie Blais Comeau ★ Etiquette Julie*, helps my email recipients quickly make the professional connection to prioritize their Inbox.

TO, CC AND BCC

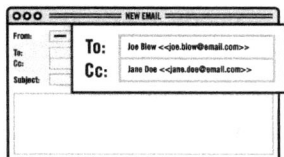

When deciding who to include as a recipient make the distinction between To and Cc (carbon copy).

Generally, To requests a reply while Cc is only FYI (For Your Information).

Be considerate of people's time by recognizing that To is equated with a reply and that replying can take longer than sending an email. When you have received a copy of an email (Cc), it is intended for your information; you are not expected to, and more importantly, should not reply. The email was not addressed to you.

When sending an email, take the time to give clear instructions for reply options. For example, "Only reply to this email *if you are not* attending the luncheon". This is a great time saving tip.

With multiple recipients, list them according to their organizational chart ranking. Start with the most senior person. The first To would be the CEO; second most important person; and so on, going from the highest to the lowest ranking.

Only send copies (Cc) to those who need to be in the loop. Sending unnecessary copies will eventually make these recipients (those unnecessarily in the Cc list) ignore your future emails. Email surveys regularly list being sent unnecessary copies as the number one pet peeve of email recipients.

At times, when using Cc, it may be best to inform the primary recipient of the reason why you added a person in Cc. For example, "Jean, I have copied Micheline on this email. She will be handling the office while I attend the Las Vegas conference. She is up to speed on your file and will know how to contact me at all times."

Only Reply All when all need to be in the know. Generally, you only need to Reply to the Sender of the email. Every click to open an email takes time. If you were part of a Reply All list of 25, for your choice of chicken or beef for the Annual Gala, you could waste 10 minutes opening and deleting data that do not require your attention or input. All of these clicks add up at the end of the week and can easily get on people's nerves.

---

[19] http://www.etiquettejulie.com/?q=story/what-do-and-say

Use the Bcc (Blind carbon copy) field when sending an email to a list of multiple recipients. If you regularly email them as a whole, create a contact group. That name will appear in the Bcc line. Clients or Newsletter is better than Undisclosed Recipients.

When using Bcc for multiple recipients, you should also fill the To section with your name. If a recipient accidentally hits Reply All you, and only you, will be receiving the message.

Use Bcc sparingly with third parties. It may be perceived as deceitful or lacking in transparency. Instead, to send a Bcc, use the Forward function. This will also give you the opportunity of adding complementary information ahead of the forwarded email.

SUBJECT

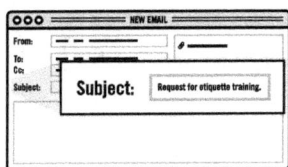

Always fill out the subject line. Some servers consider an email without a subject line as spam.

Your subject should reflect your email's content. A good subject line will allow your recipient to prioritize it. It is win-win; you get the attention that your email deserves and your recipient can quickly categorize it in his/her timeline.

Update the subject line as necessary. An expired subject line could deter the recipient from opening it in due time. A new subject line will clearly indicate your new objective and will be much more productive for all parties.

If necessary, clean up the email trail.

When your email necessitates a specific action or when you are requesting an action within a specific timeline, include that call to action in your subject line "Please reply by Friday."

GREETING

> When your email message is five words or less, place them in the subject line, followed by EOM (End Of Message). Make sure that you only use EOM with people who know what it means. The first time you use EOM, spell out the acronym.

Begin the first of every email communication with a greeting. "Dear" still is the most formal of greetings. It can be used for your clients and your boss.

Respect the company's culture. Some will prefer first names, while others insist on official and professional titles.

> For more on the proper use of titles, I recommend *Honor & Respect: The Official Guide to Names, Titles, and Forms of Address.*[20] It was written by one of my Protocol School of Washington's instructors, Robert Hickey. Robert is a very knowledge and engaging

"Good day", "Greetings" followed by "First name" or "All" can also be used as in regular email correspondence.

Avoid "Hey" adopt "Hi" followed by "First name" for close colleagues and clients.

When daily playing email Ping-Pong, going back and forth with emails, only the first email necessitates a greeting.

Because you do not know when your recipient will open his email, do not use Good morning, afternoon or evening.

BODY

Looks count. Although an email is all about words, the visual first impression of your email will impact how its' recipient views it.

Format your emails in legible, printable fonts, sizes and colours. Funky fonts or colors have no place in business correspondence. Avoid backgrounds. Make sure that whatever customization you make, that it will be as legible in print as in your email. The regular font sizes vary between 10 and 12 while the most readable colors are shades of black and blue.

Short paragraphs and sentences will broadcast professionalism and conciseness.

Take a look at the entire body of your email, from a distance to evaluate its visual appeal.

Most email messages answer what you or others will do, how it will be done and by when is it expected.

The why is the reason. It is often best to express it by phone or in person, especially when it deals with a sensitive issue. When doubtful about putting the why, the reasons behind your actions or that of others in an email, pick up the telephone or request an in person meeting.

---

[20] Robert Hickey, *Honor & Respect: The Official Guide to Names, Titles, and Forms of Address* (Columbia: Protocol School of Washington, 2008).

In emails, business casual wording is all right with internal colleagues, suppliers or clients with whom you regularly interact.

Emailing is not texting, tweeting, chatting or telegraphing. Emails should always be in the proper form. Use a spell checker, fully structured sentences, proper punctuation and capitalization for all outgoing emails.

When first introducing an acronym, follow it up with its meaning: DND (Department of National Defence).

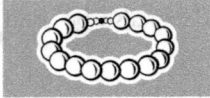

Add NNTR (No Need To Reply) to information emails that do not require a response.

When you are in doubt about the tone of an email, do not send it. Wait or ask a trusted colleague to review it.

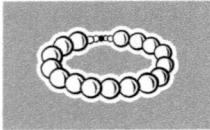

ToneCheck, a Canadian software can help you verify the tone of your email. Visit www.tonecheck.com[21]. This software works with your existing email to gauge words against connotative feelings.

Emoticons may add the missing visual clues to your messages. Use them sparingly and only with close business relations that will understand their meaning.

CLOSING

End your emails with a salutation that is in line with the subject and tone of your email. "Thank you for your time", "I look forward to collaborating with you", "At your service", "Sincerely", "Kind regards", are some of my favourites.

SIGNATURE

Your first email in the chain should contain your signature according to your company's standards, with at least: your full name, your title, the full name of your company and your telephone number with its extension. Subsequent reply emails must at minimum have your name and phone number.

Be careful about adding life quotes. Make sure that they are in line with your employer's values, and that they are allowed according to the signature standards of your organization.

---

[21] http://tonecheck.com/?__lsa=4fbf-3f9f

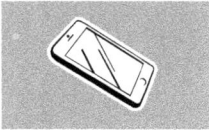

If your first name is not common, and it could cause gender confusion for the recipient, follow your name with its title abbreviation, Ms. or Mr.: Hoda Champagne (Ms.).

ATTACHMENTS

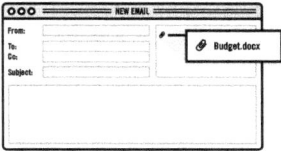

Start your email by first inputting your attachment(s). Then, fill out the To box and lastly, the subject line. This way, you will never forget attachment(s) and slow down your productivity and that of the recipient(s).

Avoid logos that appear as attachments.

In the body of your email, inform your recipient(s) of the presence of attachment(s) and the number of attachment(s).

When sending a voluminous attachment, check with the recipient first, for the size capacity of his/her account. Consider using a condensed file, a large message server like Dropbox [22] or sending multiple emails.

When sending multiple emails number them in the following manner: 1 of 4, until all have been sent: 4 of 4.

BASIC EMAIL MANNERS

Email is most likely your primary mode of communication. Some of you love listening to the patter of your keyboard and in a world where you are a click away from immortality; some precautions need to be taken.

You are at work, in front of your computer. Pick a scenario: your boss is behaving badly; your cubicle neighbor is nagging, yet again, or you wish to rekindle last night's romantic moment with your lover. You get the itch to use your computer to rhythmically vent, share or schmooze. Caution. Before you get into the action, handle with care. Danger. Red lights should be flashing. Your business email is not your personal diary.

---

[22] https://www.dropbox.com

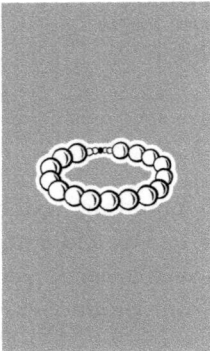

- Remember, your employer owns your business email account and can audit it at any time.

- The golden rule of email: *never send an email that you would not want seen or heard as the lead story of your favourite news source.* This includes venting, complaining, gossiping about your employer, colleagues or clients, sharing confidential information with a company outsider, abusive language or pictures, and even jokes.

- Never, ever, job search while on your company's Internet service.

Respond to all emails in a timely manner, 24 to 48 hours is the norm. If you will act on an email later, simply acknowledge its receipt by informing its sender of the expected delay for your complete response and actions. The recipient will appreciate the courteous gesture that allows him to plan accordingly.

Use read and delivery receipts only when necessary. Most people find them annoying, disrespectful and even insulting.

Use the High importance flag only when it truly is highly important.

Edit email chains. Two to three emails should suffice for ongoing matters.

Use the Auto reply feature for your absences or inability to answer emails promptly. Include your return to normal activity date along with the name and email of a contact person in your absence.

When replying to email from your mobile telephone, remove the "Sent from my Blackberry, iPhone or other" signature. This signature is advertising for your telephone company. From the recipient's perspective, your telephone's model may seem snobbish. On the other hand, he/she may be wondering why you did not wait to give the email all your attention or did not simply call.

SENDER'S REMORSE, SO REAL... ....

You have probably heard about the girl who typed swear words while describing her boss's manic demands and sent it to Susan Sharp, her boss, instead of Susan Shannon her sister. "Oh my gosh...thank God that was not me", you sigh.

There is also John, your college classmate, who works in HR for a retail company on the West Coast. When you last spoke with him, he embarrassingly confessed about his email blunder. He sent the contact list of a newly formed team to all of its members. It was on an Excel spreadsheet that also included, on p.2, all the salaries of the associates. He thought he had removed that information when he last saved the contact list.

You would never do that, would you? Could you be him?

Now, how about this one, could this be you? You receive an invitation email to the company's seasonal retreat. The organizer is your closest friend at work. You send your personal request to not be seated next to Mr. Hanes. You cannot stand his body odour. Damage is done; you pressed Reply All. Oh no, I am sure that you now want to know how you can avoid this and other electronic gaffes.

| SOLUTIONS TO RECOVER FROM EMAIL SEND SYNDROME

When you get that sinking stomach feeling

- Take responsibility. You cannot UNSEND an email; you can RECALL it, but not UNSEND it.
- Step away from your computer.
- Calm down. Have a glass of water. Wash your hands Regroup.
- Call and request an in person conversation with the recipient of your email gaffe.
- Inform the recipient that you made a terrible mistake, and that he/she will not like it.
- Depending on the situation, it may also be wise to inform your boss.
- Apologize and tell the steps, if any, that you will take to remedy the situation.
- Do not make excuses.
- Accept the consequences graciously, including a possible dismissal.
- Going forward, always check the To field.
- Going forward, always check the To field (this is not a typo, DO IT TWICE).
- Remember the golden rule of email: never send an email that you would not want seen or heard as the lead story of your favourite news source.

Email is here to stay and occupies a big chunk of your day. Go easy on yourself and go easy on others and above all, email on to others, as you would like emailed on to you. May email peace be with you.

| SOCIAL NETWORKS

> Netiquette is the contraction of Inter-net or net-work and etiquette. It encompasses the rules of interactions in emails, on social forums, blogs and any internet-based medium.
>
> –Intel broadcast of the original *Netiquette Guidelines* in 1995.

At the time that I am writing this section of my book, I may be virtually connected with you on: my personal *Facebook* timeline, my professional *Facebook page*[23], my *LinkedIn network* [24] or on my *Twitter thread*[25]. I have just begun re-pinning pictures for my dream home on *Pinterest* …ah, someday, but you do not know about it because I have not shared it with anyone…yet.

Social networks are evolving at an incredible rate. Who knows where you and I may be connected, sometime soon on a virtual network?

If we are virtually connected, you have a window into my world. You may know what book is on my bedside table, what I cooked for dinner last night, that Garde Manger's Chef, Chuck Hughes @chucksdayoff replied "Niiiiiice" to my tweet picture of his ribs recipe, where I will be giving an interactive workshop tomorrow, or you may have even seen a picture of my office and of my loved ones.

Permanent, indelible, non-erasable, immortalized, all of these adjectives describe the words, the photos, the interactions that you have on social networks. Whether you input for professional or personal purposes, they are there to stay. Is this not a scary thought?

Social networks, like after work drinks, may blur the lines between your work and play turfs. These interactive communication platforms and your life roles: child, parent, colleague, client, employee, volunteer, patient, etc. should always be coherent with your personal and professional brands.

> 70 percent of CEOs at Fortune 500 companies have no social media presence.
>
> –According to a July 2012 study sponsored by Domo and CEO.com

---

[23] www.facebook.com/EtiquetteJulieCanada?ref=hl
[24] www.linkedin.com/profile/view?id=41806307&trk=nav_responsive_tab_profile_pic
[25] www.twitter.com/EtiquetteJulie

While the settings and designs of your favourite digital network may change more quickly than your friend can remove himself from a photo where he is wearing a brief European style bathing suit, social site sharing should follow some recommendations to help you shine virtually.

REGULARLY SEARCH YOURSELF ....

You should know what is out there about you. If it is not good or out-dated: remove it, ask to have it removed or update it. When necessary contact the company, or the person that is posting. Politely request that the post be removed or that the information be updated. This includes rectifying a name search that could lead to your previous employer instead or your current one.

POLICE YOUR PROCEDURES ....

Follow your company's social networking policy.

Ask permission before posting professionally.

Write your own individual personal policy for participating in social media conversations. To establish your guidelines, answer the question "What do I want to do here and with whom?". These guidelines will help you decide when you receive an invitation to become friends or connect. They will give you the rationale to decline friends or make connections.

Respect your personal and professional brands. Respect yourself and your employer. No matter how hard you try to keep your personal and professional personas separate, they become one in the business world.

Use privacy settings to reflect your personal policy and only broadcast according to those you choose.

Prefer quality to quantity in friends, followers and connections.

Be transparent, be you and tell the truth. Most people have a tendency to be more formal at work and more casual on their Facebook page. The real you is somewhere in the middle. Handle your quest for witty comments and posts with care.

DO NOT USE AUTOMATED MESSAGES ....

When reaching out to build your network, take the time to customize your message. From the recipient's perspective, it is all about W.I.I.F.M. (What's In It For Me). Do your homework and inform the invitee why it is beneficial to connect.

PROTECT THE CONFIDENTIALITY OF YOUR NETWORK

Protect the details of your professional projects and the contact information of your colleagues, clients, even competitors, along with the privacy of your friends and loved ones.

USE COMMON SENSE, COMMON COURTESY AND CONTRIBUTE TO HARMONY...

Resist the temptation to respond in anger. You do not always need to engage. Ignoring is sometimes acceptable.

> **...The Internet's not written in pencil, Mark, it's written in ink...**
>
> –Erica Albright to Mark Zucherberg in the 2010 movie *The Social Network*

| SOLUTIONS TO STICKY SOCIAL NETWORK SITUATIONS

A client or colleague asks you to join them on a social network.

• You can ignore them. It is an option.

• You can send a message to inform:

> · the person that you prefer to connect on a professional network such as LinkedIn.

> · that you have a personal policy of not including professional connections in your online networks.

On the other hand, do not ask colleagues, clients or your boss to befriend you on Facebook. That includes no poking and no tagging.

A colleague takes a picture of you partying during your last out of town conference and posts it on his/her Facebook page and you do not approve.

• Ask them to remove it: simply, politely and firmly.

• Going forward you can decline to be included in photos. It is your choice and your job can depend on it.

On the other hand, always inform others where and by whom your photos will be seen.

Your boss has left you a message that she wants to see you first thing Monday morning. She was on Facebook and saw the photos from the previous scenario.

• Get into Facebook and remove that tag.

• While you are in there, audit your account as if you were your boss.

• Take responsibility.

• Indicate the steps you have taken to clean up your account and your act.

Remember that not everything needs to be immortalized. Let your memory remember. *Everything that happens in Vegas, stays in Vegas* and in your memory.

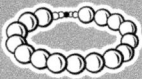

Before posting, commenting, tagging, liking or poking, do The Two Fridges Test

- Mentally put up your photos from your last weekend out with friends on your home fridge. It was a blast! It was the best time ever! Your roommate gets up, goes to the fridge for juice, sees the picture and says "Wow, great outfit. It looks like you guys had a great time". Your Mom decides to stop by to bring you lasagne. Are you comfortable with her seeing that photo? She is with your little six-year-old sister and your 66-year-old grandmother. Are you still good with them seeing that picture?

- Now take it down from your home fridge and put it up on the staff cafeteria fridge, where everyone goes to get the creamers for their coffees. Your cubicle mate is always first to get the morning coffee. He brings you a cup and says, "Where was that party? It looked like you will never forget it!" Now, big boss and little boss needed a place to talk semi-privately. They tried to go to the local coffee shop, but it was full. They decide to hold their meeting in the staff cafeteria. Are you still comfortable with them seeing the photograph of your weekend fun?

- If you give the thumbs up to both fridge posts, post it. If not, do not post.

- In my own personal and professional experience, if I have to stop and mentally ask myself, "Would this picture or comment pass the "Two Fridges Test, it more than likely does not."

| VIDEOCONFERENCES

Videoconferencing saves on travel costs, minimizes your time away from your daily routine and gives you the insight of in person meetings. So why are so many people shying away from it?

Videoconferencing is not, part telephone and part camera. Videoconferencing is more like a TV reality show, in your work world. Whether you are talking or not, the camera is recording images and sounds that are heard and seen, by all present. For many of you, that can feel weird.

To make this two-way audio-video multi location transmission a success, tune into your favourite newscast and anchorperson, for on-air guidance on how to look prepared, professional and focused. Television news people are good videoconferencing models.

PREPARED

Send the agenda ahead of time to all participants. This will allow the participants to prepare accordingly.

When deciding on a videoconference time, consider the different time zones of all participants. There are twenty-four time zones in our world.

Test the technology before the meeting. Trust me, everyone will be peeved when they hear "Can you all see the presentation?" while they've been staring at a blank screen, for the past 10 minutes. If lights, camera and action are out of your comfort zone get the support of professionals.

Lighting is crucial. Open lights, and if needed, close blinds and curtains.

Turn off all other technologies. They will distract you and the others.

Like the news show, no matter what is on your agenda, start and end on time.

PROFESSIONAL

The smallest and least visible microphone is best; more like the secret service than hanging wires and unadjusted headsets.

Make sure to mute your microphone if you sneeze, cough or blow your nose. If you are in a group setting, make sure that the microphone is in the middle of everyone present.

In the context of an in person meeting, your body language is most important. Use the posture of a news anchor. Frame the camera on your upper body.

Tidy up your desk and remove a knick-knack or two from the background if you have to.

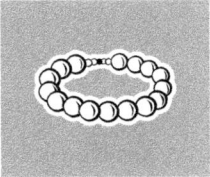

> Personally, whenever I go on camera from my home office, whether for a media contribution, a coaching session with a client, or synergizing with my master-mind group, I always have a globe, my Self-Employed Business Woman of the Year trophy, books and a plant in the background. That is my professional background.

Just like your favourite TV person, speak in your normal voice. Mute your microphone if you need to move.

While you are thinking about your favourite news anchor, emulate his/her clothing style by avoiding patterns, all black, or all white outfits. Muted colours and pastels work best on camera.

Remove dangling and noisy accessories.

When in large groups or when in front of new clients or colleagues, consider wearing name badges or having name tents in front of each participant.

There should be no side conversations or glances among colleagues.

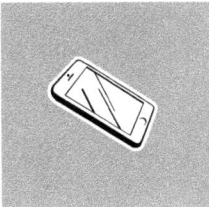

> Unlike Ron Burgundy in *Anchorman*, be prepared for a below the waist, or standing up shot. In one of the movie's posters you see the actor Will Ferrell sitting behind a news anchor desk. From above the desk, he is perfectly dressed with a suit blazer, shirt and tie. Below the desk he appears to be wearing long white boxer shorts.

FOCUSED ....

Your gaze should be directly at the camera lens when you are talking and to the screen at other times.

Do not multitask. That does include no texting, no checking messages or looking into your notebook. It is distracting and unprofessional.

Avoid relaxing habits: biting your pen, tapping your foot, picking your fingers and gum chewing. Remember you are on camera. Please do not eat.

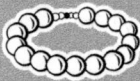

Chewing gum is relaxing and can help you remember when studying. However, when you chew it, you sometimes forget about it. The more you forget about it the more others notice it. You talk; open your mouth, gum swirls, close mouth, and repeat. Yikes!

I have already discussed my personal view on this, but it certainly is worth repeating: gum chewing should be a solitary activity, when you are alone in your office, your cubicle, or your car. At other times, prefer mints.

When the system stops:

- Let the organizer get back in touch with all the participants. Do not try to reconnect yourself.

- If you are the organizer, attempt to reconnect twice and then fall back on a teleconference. Make phone pre-arrangements for a teleconference call in case you need them.

Communication evolves. Who knows how we will be communicating by the time you pass this book onto your children or even grandchildren? One thing is for sure though, we will still be communicating with human beings, people that have agendas and have feelings.

Make it easy to communicate with you. Choose the most appropriate medium for the recipient. When in doubt ask, "How would you like me to keep you informed?" "What is the best way to reach you?" This way, you are not wasting time; your clients' or colleagues', but also yours. Respect the guidelines. When using a new medium, participate in a workshop, seek its dos and don'ts.

There is nothing more anyone that someone who repeatedly says, "I'm not good with this technology thing".We live in the digital age and it is our responsibility to learn how to contemporarily communicate. Sure, everyone will understand when you are a rookie using a new gadget but if it is part of your ongoing activities, take a class, a webinar or ask for a coaching from a colleague. Learn it.

Being an effective communicator ensures the understanding of your message by all parties. It also avoids misunderstandings; more importantly, your thoughts, ideas and opinions come across clearly to create, collaborate and cooperate.

SUMMARY

- A smile can be heard on the telephone.
- Your posture affects the sound of your voice.
- Use your mobile telephone as you would a pay booth; someone is waiting and listening.
- Remember, the Internet is not written in pencil, it is written in ink.
- Define your personal social network policy and stick to it.
- Do The Two Fridges Test before posting online.
- Videoconferencing is like reality TV; you are always on.

One of the most important business places where technology meets communication is during meetings. Let us continue getting you the career of your dreams with confidence and credibility by having an active and professional, but also productive participation in meetings.

PROFESSIONALISM GUIDELINE #5
PARTICIPATE MEANINGFULLY IN MEETINGS

A re meetings a waste of time or an inspiring and cohesive collaborative venture? What do you think?

Actually, the success of a meeting depends on the host and you. Yes, even as a participant you have a responsibility to make meetings meaningful.

You can do this by following these four guidelines.

Each guideline has best practices for when you are the Host 🔔 and when you are a Participant ✋.

| GUIDELINE #1: PURPOSE + PRODUCTS = AGENDA

🔔 If you do not have a purpose for the meeting, and you do not have intended products—expected results to come out of that meeting, do not hold a meeting.

Just because you hold a meeting every Wednesday morning, does not mean that you have to hold one when there is nothing new. Let me assure you; everyone will roll their eyes when you start the meeting with "Does anyone have anything new to report" or " Does anyone have something they want to talk about?"

Your meeting's purpose and its expected products, should guide you in planning your agenda. It should answer the questions "Why are we having the meeting?" and "What deliverables do we want to come out of it?" When stating the purpose and the products of your meeting, be as specific and as realistic as possible. Use verbs and include numbers, dates, along with your team members' names when appropriate.

Use a meeting agenda template for all meetings. It will facilitate record keeping and referencing. It will also begin the implementation process of actions. Simply carry over meeting points to form a project action plan.

In my role as human resources manager, I was a stickler for this tool. By the time I left my position, it was part of the company's culture. It made everyone's life easier and every meeting so much more productive; everyone knew what to do, and when.

I share these templates with you in the next pages. Adapt them to suit your needs and adopt them for any kind of meeting. With these tools as the basis of your meetings, you are on your way to purposeful and productive meetings.

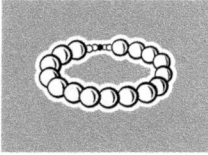

Add techno gadgets expectations at the bottom of the agenda and review them at the start of the meeting. Make sure to include guidelines that relate to social networking like: Twitter, #hashtags, smart phones, recordings, photos and laptops.

Send the agenda a couple of days ahead to solicit feedback and gain inputs.

MEETING TEMPLATE

Meeting date and location		Start and end time	
Participants list			
Please print: First name and last name		**Signature**	
1			
2			
3			
4			
5			
6			
7			
8			
9			
10			
11			
12			

Note: Please put all techno gadgets on 'Silent' mode.

Excerpt from ***ETIQUETTE: CONFIDENCE & CREDIBILITY***

MEETING TEMPLATE

Purpose of the meeting – Why are we having a meeting?		
PRODUCTS OF THE MEETING What do we want to accomplish during this meeting? Be specific by including actions, numbers, names, etc. 1. 2. 3.		
Agenda Points	**Time**	**Speaker**

Date meeting record sent			
Attached meeting record	Yes ☐	No ☐	
Attached action plan	Yes ☐	No ☐	

Meeting host signature	Date
Meeting note-taker signature	Date

Excerpt from *ETIQUETTE: CONFIDENCE & CREDIBILITY*

| GUIDELINE #2: RECORD AND DO NOT REWIND UNTIL AFTER THE MEETING

On time meeting attendees agree and I am sure that you do too; it is annoying and disrespectful when a meeting host repeats his intro for every latecomer… arghhh… Repeating—rewinding, for "Tardy Tammy or Tommy" is counter productive and puts the focus on them instead of on the meeting. Do not accommodate tardiness.

🔔 Before the start of the meeting, assign a note-keeper or record a transcript of the meeting on an electronic device. Some work teams have a rotation, while others permanently assign this role as soon as the team is formed.

The record of your meeting should reflect the meeting's purpose and products.

An action plan in the form of a table that includes what, who, how, which and when columns work well to track the progress of projects.

- **What** will be done?
- **Who** will do this?
- **How** will they do it?
- **Which** resources will be needed?
- **When** do we want this done?

For example:

What?	Who?	How?	Which?	When?
Send out the meeting invitation	Chris	By Email	Email addresses of all participants from HR	1 week before meeting

Within 24 hours of the meeting, circulate the meeting's notes or its transcript to all attendees and to those who could not make it.

Take the time to review your meeting and do a post-mortem for best practices. What went well? What could be improved on? What should we stop doing?

🖐 Do what you said that you would do and what you were assigned to do, in the designated time. Act this way on a regular basis and you will display integrity.

When meeting with one person: in person, on the phone or in a videoconference, do not ask him/her to send you an email with tasks or products from the meeting. Be accountable for what you said you would do. Take your own notes and do it. The other person's time is just as valuable as yours.

| GUIDELINE #3: ATTEND AND TEND TO THE AGENDA

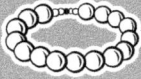

> Add freshness to your meetings by changing locations and treats.

Be realistic about your agenda and its timeline. Allow ample time for discussion, questions and answers. If it is necessary, give time limits to brainstorming and individual sharing of ideas.

If you are preparing the agenda, invite only those that need to be there and make sure that the decision makers are present

Outlook is great tool to invite attendees and update meetings. It also allows you to add participants and make changes to the location or time and any other necessary information by pressing 'Send Update'. When cancelling a meeting, delete it from your calendar and press 'Send Cancellation'. All invitees can then 'Remove from Calendar' in just one click.

When you receive a meeting invitation, 'Accept' to confirm your attendance or 'Decline' to inform your absence, as soon as possible. This is not an option. If you cannot attend, explain the reason. A telephone call is usually best. It allows you to privately give details of your absence to the meeting's host. Typically, not all attendees need to know why you cannot go. 'Tentative' is usually the only reply that will necessitate 'Respond With Comments', like a scheduling conflict. For other reasons, here too a phone call may be a better option.

Print the meeting's agenda and make notes before the meeting, by inputting what and where you wish to contribute.

Bring all the necessary documents to the meeting: status updates, suggestions, recommendations and your copy of the agenda with your notes.

Bring note-taking materials. I know that this seems elementary but believe me; it is not obvious to all. I regularly encounter people that attend meetings without the basic meeting tools. Too many times I have had to rip a couple of pages from my notebook and search through my bag for an extra pen for someone. The empty handed attendees could not even write a note to themselves for an assigned meeting task. Really!

Pen and paper is the least distracting note-taking method. When you are using a techno gadget, make sure that it is acceptable for the host and stick to your task. No peeking at your email or texting. All can tell when you mentally steer away from the meeting.

Participate according to the agenda and your notes. If you do not have anything to say, do not waste time rephrasing what others have said. Acknowledge what others are saying with positive facial expressions and supportive comments.

Keep your body language professional. Do not sprawl on the desk and do not remove your shoes. Yes, I have witnessed this sight and that smell too. Neither was very pleasant. These behaviours take away confidence and credibility.

Also, beware of relaxing fidgety movements like the clicking of your pen or the back and forth of your foot. What may be relaxing to you may be annoying to others. I am sure that you can think of at least a couple of little irritating habits that your colleagues have. Be careful that yours don't become more than a little niggle.

Mind your meeting manners; be polite, courteous and respectful of other's ideas. Do not interrupt and please do not have side conversations. Avoid the rolling of the eyes, sighs and finger pointing. Play nice and be fair.

| GUIDELINE #4: START, SIT AND STAY FOCUSED

🔔 As soon as you get to the room evaluate the temperature. Consider that when the room is full, the ideal room temperature is 20 degrees Celsius.

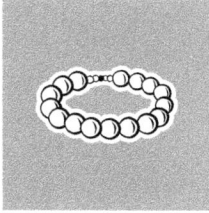

> Rumour has it that Garth Brooks, the retired American Country Music Artist would always take a seat in the bleachers during his band's rehearsals. He wanted to make sure that all would see and hear a great show. If this great entertainer could do it, we can too. Make sure that all meeting attendees have an unobstructed view of all.

Start your meeting on time, whether or not all the participants are present. If you do not, your attendees will assume it is acceptable for them to be late the next time you host a meeting.

Once you start do not stop. Latecomers can catch up by looking at their agendas or by reading the notes on the freshly passed tablet --see tip below. Never rewind the meeting.

> **If your team can never start meetings on time** because there are too many latecomers, play "Take the tablet".
>
> The host ceremoniously passes on a digital tablet or a pad of paper and pen, from the official note-taker to the last person who walks through the door. Every other person that comes in thereafter gets the ceremonial passing of the note-taking material.
>
> As a bonus for the meeting host, who does not want to rewind —repeat, the meeting to answer: "What did I miss?" the new note-taker can catch up on the status of the meeting, by reading the notes on the tablet.

Aim to finish your meeting 10 minutes early. Everyone will be thrilled with the extra time to freshen up, make a call or catch up on email. At the latest, end at the expected time.

Facilitate the meeting by involving others on the agenda's topics. Call on your in-room experts by soliciting the feedback of the other attendees.

> **Remember that a man's name is to him the sweetest and most important sound in any language.**
> –Dale Carnegie *How to win friends and influence people* [26]

If you know that your team likes to socialize before a meeting, input that time in the agenda.

8:50 to 9:00 — Muffins and Mingling

9:03 — Start meeting with agenda item #1

Start a meeting at an off-hour. Participants will be curious. They will want to be there on time to verify that you do begin at this unusual start time.

Assign strategic seating with name tents. The host, the chairperson, or the highest person in the pecking order, will be at the end of a rectangular table, with a view of the door. In this position, the meeting leader can clearly see everyone in attendance and incoming participants.

The second most important person will be directly across from the meeting leader, also to provide a good view of all participants.

The place of honour, as in social situations, is to the right. This seat could be assigned to a client, trusted advisor or visitor. The seat to the left is strategically assigned according to hierarchy and to simplify communication between decision makers.

Keep in mind that round tables facilitate brainstorming and participant interactions. Tables placed in the letter 'U' shape, promote an open forum to give a lively discussion and direct eye contact with all participants.

If your meetings always extend past the assigned time

Use a countdown clock and make it visible to all. Especially look at it when transitioning from one agenda point to the next. This tactic is also effective when a participant lingers with comments.

When brainstorming, use an hourglass or a talking stick—only the person holding it can speak.

Park items that are not on the agenda and that need to be addressed later in a *Parking lot*—participants write the out of agenda items on the assigned flip chart, the white board or on sticky notes, and post them well in sight for all to see, at the front of the room. Make sure to review these at the end of the meeting to: give answers, assign tasks, give a timeline or transfer them to the next meeting's agenda.

---

[26] Carnegie Dale. *How to win friends and influence people* (New York: Simon and Schuster, 1936).

✋ Arriving on time at a meeting means no earlier than 10 minutes before its start time. This gives the host or organizers all the space they need to set up successfully without worrying about people's presence and entertaining them while waiting for all to show up.

If you roll in late, do not shake papers and do not rattle your chair. Settle in, listen and look at your copy of the agenda to pick up with the momentum. A quick, "Excuse me" will do for now. After the meeting, you may privately apologize to the host and explain further.

Respect assigned seating. When seating is not assigned, do not sit on the ends of the table or to the right or left of these chairs. They are usually for the host, guest of honour or key people, and their assistants.

Stay in the meeting; do not go in and out. If you need to leave early or to excuse yourself for a predetermined important activity, make sure to inform the host before the start of the meeting. When leaving, do so as quietly as possible.

Productive meetings are appreciated by all and give focus to teams and organizations.

Running effective meetings is much more than sending out an invitation to gather around for a nice cup of coffee and pretty cupcakes to talk about our big plan. Productive meetings require preparation, planning, positive and purposeful participation, post-meeting actions, and performance analysis. More importantly productive meetings do not waste precious time and resources.

SUMMARY

- Every meeting needs a purpose and expected products. Together they form the agenda.
- Send the agenda ahead of time.
- Do not be late, stay focused and on time.
- Track meetings products with standardized templates that include what, who, how, which and when.

Participating according to meeting rules will definitely contribute to the overall workplace atmosphere.

In the next chapter, we will expand on the subject of workplace civility. I will empower you with how to take an empathetic approach to your workplace. This will ultimately allow you to benefit from an increase in productivity.

CONTRIBUTE TO CIVILITY @ WORK

> *Please be polite. Nothing in life should erode the habit of saying thank you to people or praising them.*
>
> –Sir Richard Branson, Founder and Chairman, Virgin Group

| BAD BUSINESS BEHAVIOUR IS BAD FOR THE BOTTOM LINE

Bad business behaviour is more than bad manners; it is bad for the bottom line.

Find out why rudeness is expensive. In the chart below, connect the letters to the numbers; the percentages to the statements. This activity unveils the cost of incivility according to the book, *The Cost of Bad Behaviour: How Incivility Is Damaging Your Business and What to Do About It*[27] by Christine Pearson and Christine Porath.

1. Employees lost work time worrying about the incident	A. 38%
2. Employees decreased their work effort	B. 47%
3. Employees said their performance declined	C. 48%
4. Employees decreased their work quality	D. 63%
5. Employees lost time avoiding their offender	E. 66%
6. Employees decreased their time at work	F. 78%
7. Employees said that their commitment to the organization declined.	G. 80%

Answer key: 1 = G, 2 = C, 3 = E, 4 = A, 5 = D, 6 = B, 7 = F

---

[27] Christine Pearson and Christine Porath, *The Cost of Bad Behaviour: How Incivility Is Damaging Your Business and What to Do About It* (New York: Portfolio/Penguin 2009).

As you can now attest from the above connections, incivility is costly for us all. It affects you, your productivity and ultimately, your team's results. Lost time is lost money. More importantly, worry takes its toll on you and your health. When you are unhealthy, you are not a productive employee. Bad behaviour is bad for business.

CIVILITY SELF-EVALUATION

Could you be "that guy" or "that girl" that disrupts workplace harmony? Every work environment has at least one of these employees. He/she is the kind of person that nobody dares to name. All refer to him/her as "that guy" or "that girl". Could you be the one offending team members, without knowing about it or even intending to? Find out in this next exercise, for your eyes only, from the *Thunderbird School of Global Management*[28]. In the first column, check what you have witnessed. In the second column, check what you may have done. Include the unintentional ones too.

	Incivility in action	Others	You
1	Taking credit for others' efforts		
2	Passing blame for your own mistakes		
3	Checking email or texting during a meeting		
4	Sending bad news through an e-mail so you do not have to face the recipient		
5	Talking down to others		
6	Not listening		
7	Spreading rumours about colleagues		
8	Setting others up for failure		
9	Not saying "please" or "thank you"		
10	Showing up late or leaving a meeting early with no explanation		
11	Belittling others' efforts		
12	Leaving snippy voice mail or email messages		
13	Forwarding others' email to make them look bad		
14	Making demeaning or derogatory remarks to someone		
15	Withholding information		
16	Failing to return telephone calls or respond to email		
17	Leaving a mess for others to clean up		
18	Consistently grabbing easy tasks while leaving difficult ones for others		
19	Shutting someone out of a network or team		
20	Paying little attention or showing little interest in others' opinions		

[28] http://www.thunderbird.edu/article/cost-bad-behavior-how-incivility-damaging-your-business

Excerpt from *ETIQUETTE: CONFIDENCE & CREDIBILITY*

Workplace incivility is not bullying. It is often the result of that guy, or that girl's, one bad day and their individual one choice, not to care or not to listen.

It could be as simple as not using the magic words "please", "thank you", "hello" or "I am sorry". It may be as distracting as that guy constantly checking his PDA (Personal Digital Assistant) for emails or texting during a presentation. It can also be as frustrating as that girl taking credit for someone else's idea or passing blame for her own mistake. It is as subtle as his sigh, her roll of the eyes and withholding information. It could even be as damaging as that guy making a demeaning or derogatory remark to someone.

There are times when it affects more than one person, like when a meeting leader has to repeat the entire introduction and agenda because that girl is late again. Or when she does not hand in her part of the project on time.

Sometimes, it is not even work related. The consequences of these unofficial actions certainly impact workplace harmony, like when that guy leaves a mess for others to clean up.

If no one acknowledges workplace incivility, it cannot be corrected. Start now by acknowledging your own behaviour.

Even the most considerate of employees can have a blind spot, so ask a trusted colleague if you have little annoying habits that could be exasperating other team members. A little niggle for you, could be a big pet peeve to a co-worker.

Think about the consequences of your own words and actions. Demonstrate empathy. Ask yourself, "How will my colleague, my assistant, my cubicle neighbour feel if I say or do _____?" By filling in the blank and walking in your teammate's shoes, you will most likely follow through with civil conduct. Just treat others and their workspaces, as you would like to be treated.

| DON'T BE THAT GUY OR THAT GIRL, BE THE ONE

> *I propose that as a society, we take a new, close look at that intriguing code of behaviour based on respect, restraint and responsibility that we call civility.*
>
> –P.M. Forni, a professor of Italian Literature at John Hopkins University and author of *Choosing Civility: The Twenty-Five Rules Of Considerate Conduct* [29]

Do you ever feel like standing on top of your desk to belt out Aretha Franklin's anthem, *R-E-S-P-E-C-T* to "that guy" or "that girl"? Sadly, you are not alone. Office manners are declining while workplace woes are rising.

Although you may wish you could, by respect for yourself and for your employer, you press forward on the queen of soul's album and instead hum *I Say a Little Prayer*. To the rhythm of the gospel blues, you choose to show restraint, take a deep breath, count to ten or go for a walk. In that one moment, you are making the one choice to be civil. It only takes one: one moment, one choice and one person to initiate civility.

I believe in the power of one, you. I am not saying that you should walk around with a civility badge on and a pad ready to hand out incivility tickets to whoever lacks respect, restraint or responsibility. I am simply saying that acknowledgement of your own actions will have an impact. Easier said than done, you may be thinking. Allow me to enlighten you. When you are aware, you respect others, their values and their things. You also restrain yourself from hurting them, and you take responsibility for your actions.

Civility is contagious. Others will observe, notice and even imitate your actions. You have the power to inspire others to contribute to civility.

As the basis of our universal code of behaviour, Dr. Forni states *The Twenty-five Rules of Considerate Conduct*. I recommend that you read his book and maybe even share it with your team. Let Dr. Forni's list guide you and inspire you.

Whenever I deliver a workshop on workplace civility, I randomly assign 25 participants to read these rules. After they have been enunciated aloud, there is always a tranquil calmness in the room. People smile, nod, and agree with what their peers have read.

---

[29] P.M. Forni, *Choosing Civility: The Twenty-five Rules of Considerate Conduct*. (New York: St Martin's Press 2002)

PROFESSIONALISM GUIDELINE #6 **YOU AT YOUR BEST @ WORK** | 143

Common courtesy seems so simple, but as you may have experienced, common courtesy is not common sense.

If only all your coworkers and clients acted with respect, restraint, and responsibility, what a wonderful world your work world would be. Once again, I believe that it all starts with the power of one, one choice. Choose to contribute to civility and manage your relationships with good intentions, actions, and emotions, one choice at a time. Do good, and feel good.

Respect starts with self-respect. You accept yourself just the way you are. You like you without comparing. This translates into confident behaviour. Accept and value others and their contributions in the same manner.

Respecting does not mean tolerating, especially in the presence of uncivil conduct. In such a case, do not point fingers. Instead, express your needs in a firm but calm voice. You know the one; the non-judgemental, sensible and sensitive voice. It clearly displays restraint from anger and takes responsibility for consequences. For example, when three colleagues are talking in the hallway, simply state "I need to focus on this report and I am having a hard time concentrating. I would really appreciate it if you could please take your discussion elsewhere, so I can get back to my work." No one is belittled and relationships can continue to evolve positively without resentment.

You have heard this many times before, and it is true: "You cannot change others. The only person you can change is you." Once again, the power of one; it starts with you.

By its word origin, civility reminds us to be good citizens and good neighbours and this applies to your office, your team, your organization, your firm, or your clinic, and especially in your cubicle dwelling when you are in such close proximity to your teammates.

So, the next time that you feel like standing on top of your desk and belting out *R-E-S-P-E-C-T*, switch the track to the Spice Girls. "Stop, right now, thank you very much, be the one with the human touch. Don't be 'those guys' on the run. Slow it down. Be the one and maybe have some fu-uun."

| THE 3 Ss OF SENSORY ETIQUETTE: SIGHTS, SMELLS & SOUNDS

Your office, with your personal belongings and a picture of your loved ones, may feel a lot more like the set of *Big Brother* than your private sanctuary for creativity and productivity.

Whether you work in a small mom and pop family-owned business or a big Fortune 500 company's headquarters, chances are that you do not have a corner office with a window. Like most of the office workers that you know, you probably work in a cubicle.

With walls shorter than the average person, no ceiling as a buffer and no door for privacy, yours and your cubicle neighbours' sights, smells and sounds cross over personal boundaries to, at times, distract the professional flow of business.

Biggest pet peeves in the place of business:

- Loud talkers is 32%
- Cell phones ringing is 30%
- Speakerphone use in public areas is 22%
- Personal conversations is 11%
- Personal digital assistants during meetings is 9%

–Harris Interactive (R) for Randstad's monthly Job Bites surveyed 2 318 employees on workplace etiquette in 2006

It is a fact that your cubicle neighbour's ring tone, perfume, gum chewing or pencil tapping are just little niggles that can become annoyances and ultimately hinder your productivity.

Without a traditional door to give you privacy, office cubicles are open to visual scrutiny by all, at all times. You may even feel like you are working in a fish bowl.

As you are typing away at your desk, colleagues on their way to a meeting in the boardroom, to the washroom or out to lunch, discreetly peek into your work world. Based on what they see: your pile of papers, your shoe collection or the contents of your opened drawer, they form impressions of you and your work habits.

You also judge them on what you see in their quarters but also on what you hear and what you smell coming from their workstations. What is irritating you is likely irritating your neighbours too.

To be an active contributor to a respectful workplace environment, be aware of the sensory annoyances that you may be sending out. Self-awareness and prevention are the keys to civility.

Here are 15 Cubicle Courtesies. Follow them and you are sure to get the Cubicle Dweller of the Year award.

THE SIGHTS

Decorate and upkeep your office in the same manner that your company's highest-ranking person does.

1. Choose your screen saver wisely. Does it represent the professional image you wish to broadcast and is it in line with your employer's values?

2. Limit your personal objects to your most-recent diploma, a photo, a mirror, a plant and one significant knick-knack. Your cubicle decorations should not contain offensive messages that could be misinterpreted. That includes sarcastic cartoons or funny quotations.

3. Add a hook on top of one of your cubicle's walls for your coat, a jacket or the wrap that you keep for colder days.

4. Do not display your shoes at the office. It is distracting and could even be unsafe. If you keep more than one pair of shoes at the office place them neatly under your desk or in a drawer.

5. At the end of your day, leave an organized workspace. Should you unexpectedly be absent tomorrow, your space will send out the right message.

How you keep your desk influences what other people think of you.

- 57% have judged coworkers on how clean or dirty they keep their work spaces.
- 42% have judged coworkers more negatively if their workspaces are dirty.
- 45% have judged coworkers more positively if their work spaces are clean.
- 42% think a dirty work space is a result of employees simply being too busy.
- 33% think messy employees are lazy employees.
- 73% think people are most productive when their work spaces are clean.

–Adecco Survey of 1015 employees

THE SOUNDS ....

Avoid listening in. If you happen to hear personal, confidential information, keep it to yourself.

6. Use appropriate tone and words.

7. Turn off the sound of your technological gadgets. Vibration does make a sound, and it too can be distracting. Use a headset for your computer's sounds.

8. Make personal calls at break time in a private space.

9. Minimize nervous sounds, like the clicking of a pen. They may be a stress reliever for you, but they can distract your neighbours. This includes nail clipping. Huhhh huhhh, I have seen this done... Even when your neighbours don't visually catch you in the act, they will recognize the sound. It violates Rule #15 *Respect other people's space* of *The Twenty-five Rules of Considerate Conduct*.

10. Instead of being a Jack in the Box, talking above the cubicle wall, visit and call your neighbours or send them an email or a text.

THE SMELLS ....

Control your odours, even the natural ones.

11. Avoid eating in your cubicle; especially hot foods. Cooked aromas travel fast.

12. Discard food items and snacks in eating areas. Leftovers have lingering smells.

13. Be careful with perfume and cologne, less is more. If you smell them on yourself, you are wearing too much. Prefer air neutralizers to air fresheners and pot-pouri. If you are not sure about an odour, ask your neighbour(s) first.

14. Freshen up in designated areas; the washroom or the gym.

15. Keep your shoes on your feet. Put your gym shoes in a bag under your desk or in a drawer with a sheet of laundry softener.

You spend most of your waking days at work with your cubicle colleagues. Do yourself and your team a favour, talk to your boss or human resources to plan a brainstorming session to make your own Cubicle Code of Conduct for a productive, creative and efficient work environment for all.

| SOLUTIONS TO PROTECT YOUR PRIVATE PRODUCTIVITY SPACE

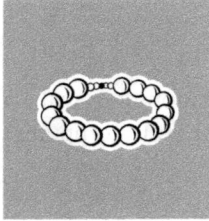

- Just as you would knock before entering when there is an office door, check to make sure that your colleague is available for your visit.

- To inform colleagues of your visiting availability, make and post on your wall, a reversible sign (similar to the ones used in hotels) to signal, "Do not disturb" or "Please come in". Turn it over as your day evolves.

To tell or not to tell your cubicle neighbour that he/she

- Has a body odour?
- Constantly chews and cracks gum?
- Taps his/her foot on the leg of his desk?
- Clips his/her toenails?

Most employees do not intend on grossing out or distracting their colleagues. A lot of the time they are unaware of the ripple effects of their actions.

As a rule, people want to be liked, so an honest conversation will most likely be appreciated by your teammate. Note that conversations that have to do with personal hygiene and grooming are best held with members of the same sex.

- Invite your colleague to a private area for a conversation. This is crucial. It has to be away from other's eyes and ears.

- Start your conversation with a few words of appreciation for your colleague's input into the team and your appreciation of your collaboration.

- Mention that what you are about to say is difficult to talk about but that if the roles were reversed, you would appreciate the honesty instead of being part of the office gossip.

- If appropriate, as in the case of body odor, mention the uncontrollable, physical effects that stress can have on the body.

As with most work situations, entrusting the task to your superior or HR is usually a good decision. In today's culturally diverse workplace, depending on your colleague, this could also be the safest alternative. If you are not sure about your relationship to this person or your choice of words, this is the way to go. You certainly would not want to be perceived as harassing someone.

| THE MAGIC WORDS

"Give me that stapler." "Have that report on my desk by Monday morning." "Pass that document—with pointing eyes and finger at the piece of paper on top of your pile." Do you notice anything missing in these co-worker interactions? The magic words are missing. I am not referring to "abracadabra" or to "open sesame." I am referring to the very first words that you probably learned. They allowed you to get the extra cookie or that special treat that you loved so much. You have known them since you could speak; "Please" and "Thank you." From toddlerhood, these words are ingrained in our brains to demonstrate gratitude, appreciation and acknowledgement of others' actions and gifts.

Recently, it seems that in the name of productivity and efficiency, the polite words have completely vanished from the modern workplace.

Our speedy casual contemporary language has also dropped "You are welcome" and in some instances, it has been replaced by the very popular "No problem." This is a pet peeve of mine. "No problem" they say. Well, I was not aware that there was a problem. It particularly niggles at me, when I say "Thank you for returning a telephone call or for accepting an invitation" and they reply "No problem". There is not a problem here. Saying thank you is a courtesy. The correct response is "You are welcome."

Granted, greetings and sayings have evolved. In the 1956 Broadway musical *My Fair Lady*, Professor Higgins taught Eliza Doolittle, the Cockney flower girl, to reply, "How do you do." when she was introduced to high-society ladies and gentlemen. Notice, that her phrase does not end with a question mark but with a period. With this phrasing and the correct accent, she could pass off as a well-born lady.

These days, when being introduced, the more common response is "Hello, how are you." or even "Hi, how is it going." Both phrases are also not true questions but more of a meeting formality.

Respect for others can be evidenced by different words and actions. When you get to work, to Ms. CEO, you may say "Good morning ma'am" with a sincere polite smile and discreet eye contact. And to your best work buddy, you probably say something like "Hey bud, how's it going." with a big smile, the thumb up gesture and direct eye contact as your eyebrows slightly rise.

Words and gestures adapt to the workplace culture, the environment and the hierarchy of the people you encounter.

"Hello" is another magic word. "Hi", is also on that list. By using a greeting you are acknowledging the other person. It is a simple question of respect. The nod or the wave in passing in the hallway, also counts. These gestures have the same regards that are associated with the words. Not using them could quickly get you the not a team player tag. Greeting colleagues is basic courtesy, not rocket science but definitely necessary.

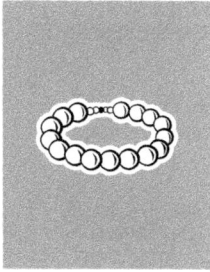

When entering your place of business, it is your responsibility to greet others as you walk in, make your way to your office or cross colleagues in the hall.

When a guest or a visitor shows up at your place of work, you will be the first to say, "Welcome," "Hello" or "Good morning." Even when you are not the first employee who he/she crosses, you will still acknowledge every visitor, in the same manner that you would greet all visitors in your home.

Salutations also apply to telephone and email communications. Before identifying yourself and/or making a request, acknowledge all callers and email recipients with a greeting.

The vocal communication of the civil workplace is inspired by a four-letter word, K-I-N-D. Use kind words in your verbal exchanges. They too have magical powers in creating courteous and civil corporate exchanges.

Compliments are kind words. Add them to your thank yous to display your appreciation "Thank you for handing your report on time Robert. I really enjoyed reading it and appreciated the statistics that support your theory." "Good morning Marie-France. That was a great presentation you did yesterday."

Apologizing at work

"I am sorry" are powerful magical words.

Unless you are a saint you will, at some point in your career, have to apologize. Apologizing heals wounds and in certain circumstances, may even protect you and your employer from liability.

- Apologize as soon as possible. The longer you wait, the more difficult it becomes and the more resentment can settle in.

- Explain clearly what you did. Don't rush. Give details as to why it was wrong. Do not give excuses. Show remorse.

- Take responsibility. "I am sorry. I feel bad for what I did to you." Tone is very important. Be sincere and empathetic. Take whatever comes after that. Absorb, observe and learn.

- Make it right by asking how you can make it right. Do whatever needs to be done to repair and maybe even compensate. Be genuine in what you can do.

- Do not lie. Be realistic.

- Do not do it again.

Never underestimate the power of The Magic Words. Do not take them for granted. Magic Words make you, and others feel good. Feel their power.

SUMMARY

- Civility starts with you.
- Civility at work involves all of the senses.
- Have an empathetic perception on your words and actions. Place yourself in the other person's shoes; listen to your words and watch your actions through the other's ears, eyes and nose.
- "Hello", "please", "thank you" and "I am sorry" are powerful words. Use them.

Interestingly, one of the few places when it is not necessary to say, "Thank you" is at the restaurant. Every time the service personnel brings or removes something from the table, you do not have to. Saying "Thank you", at the end of the meal, to accompany your tip, suffices. The reason is simple: too many thank yous create too many interruptions, especially during a business meal. Read on for more on dining.

DO NOT DO LUNCH TO EAT AND DRINK

his is probably where you thought that I would tell you all about being born with a silver spoon in my mouth. How I instinctively knew about all of the mechanics of fine dining by observing guests at fancy dinners. Well, no. That was not I. I am from an average family that shared most meals at home, away from the tra la la of banquets and galas.

I learned table manners at dinnertime. My mother was a stickler for proper table manners, especially on Sunday nights, when we visited or hosted our grandparents.

Sunday night dinner was a big deal back then. The best dinnerware we owned was perfectly laid out on an immaculate white tablecloth that had been ironed and starched. Out came the fine china, the crystal glasses and the boxed set of utensils that had been offered as a wedding gift. We even dressed up; dresses for the ladies and suits for the men. Keep in mind, that at the time, stores were closed and extracurricular activities were never scheduled on Sundays. Sunday was a day for rest and family.

These days, Sunday is just like any other day of the week. Most modern families rarely have the time to gather everyone to eat together. And when they do, they are too busy catching up and getting ready for the next activity on their list to have a teaching moment. Some parents don't even have confidence in their own dining skills to teach them to their children. You would be amazed at how many adults come up to me after my dining etiquette activities to tell me that they had no idea how to properly cut with a knife and fork, or how to hold a wine glass.

If you were not taught dining etiquette, the following scene will most likely resonate with you.

"How about lunch?" asks Mr. Client. "Oh…OK", you nervously answer. "Next Wednesday, I'll make a reservation at Chez Pierre", he invites.

How do you feel? Excited at the prospect of getting to know him better or nervous about all the fuss that Chez Pierre is known for?

Is your mind racing back to the *Pretty Woman* empty ballroom scene or to

The *Blues Brothers* Chez Paul scene? Are you just like Vivian (Julia Robert's character in *Pretty Woman*), trying to remember which fork to use first? Or, are you confidently oblivious, just like *Jack and Elwood* (John Belushi and Dan Ackroyd's characters in *The Blues Brothers*) throwing grapes into each other's mouths while making uninvited conversation with their table neighbours?

The dinner table is a great place to learn about one's social intelligence. Every year some of Canada's most prestigious law firms contract me to host etiquette dinners. They invite prospective summer students and interns to interact with their firm's senior partners. During a four-course meal, the lawyers observe how the potential employees respond to my tutorial, mingle with their tablemates, answer questions, and interact with the service personnel. Through conversation, they learn about their backgrounds, family history and interests. Interpersonal skills are a great indicator of the ability to build lasting and loyal relationships.

Your goal is for Mr. Client to say to Ms. Boss "Wow that employee is smart and pleasant too. We had a great time last night Chez Pierre." Instead of "Yeah, that employee is smart but ouch…a little dining etiquette could do a lot for him. I had a hard time focusing with all the caveman manoeuvres. He kept on talking with his mouth full, about his Vegas vacation, he never asked me a single question and yuck, he even blew his nose with his napkin!"

The secret to a successful business meal is to understand that you are not invited to satisfy your thirst or hunger. You are invited to be acquainted, to celebrate, to be thanked or hopefully to seal the deal.

The last thing that you want is to go to dinner and embarrass yourself or your employer. You want to be remembered for the right reason; you are good at what you do.

This chapter will give you the ins and outs of table manners. Your dining companions will hear what you say and notice your confidence. Gone will be the distractions that come from your hesitant utensil manoeuvres.

Do not go to a business meal hungry. You do not know when you will actually be eating. Because you have a dinner reservation at 6:00 p.m. does not mean that you will be eating shortly thereafter. There may be cocktails and there may be small talk or even business talk before the meal. Eat a little something before you go to soothe your stomach and your nerves. Have a power snack of cheese and crackers, half a bagel with cream cheese or a mini protein bar.

It is also a good idea to have a power snack before a cocktail get together with work mates. This will slow down the alcohol digestion and will keep you from being lightheaded.

| BE A GRACIOUS HOST

When you are hosting, you are responsible for all the business-dining arrangements. For a dinner invitation, you should generally send your invitation one week ahead of your selected date. For lunch or breakfast, two to three days will do.

Whether it is during an in person meeting, a telephone conversation, or in an email, make it clear that you are inviting your guest by stating the obvious: "I would like to invite you to dinner." Refrain from casual invitations without the verb invite. They will leave your guests wondering about the payment responsibility.

An invitation means that you will be paying. Paying is synonymous with inviting. This also applies to attendance at a sports or cultural event. The host pays for all that is associated with the activity during their time together. For example, if you were inviting an out-of-town guest to golf, you would pay for the rentals, the caddy, the cart, the after golf drinks and the meal.

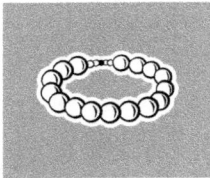

> As the organizer of a group meal, when you do not intend on paying for the group, you could say, "We are all going out for lunch on Friday. We would love for you to join us." This casual request to join a group for a meal indicates that each person will individually be paying for his/her meal.

As the host, you also want to make sure that your guests will be comfortable in the restaurant of your choice. It is therefore, your responsibility to ask about food allergies. Notice that the restaurant choice is yours, not your client's. You want to be in control of all of the elements. You don't want any surprises. If you are concerned about your guest's dislikes, give a choice of two or three restaurants.

> When sending an email meal invitation, add the hyperlink to the website of the restaurant. Your guest will be able to review the menu, directions and maybe even parking options.

It is also a good idea to select a convenient location for your client, not too far from his/her place of work.

Validate meal duration expectations, prior to the start of the meal. You can even inquire when you make the invitation. A typical business dinner is approximately two to three hours. Lunch is around an hour and a half while a breakfast meeting is expected to evolve over an hour.

Choose a restaurant that you are familiar with and especially one where the personnel knows you as a good patron. To establish a mutual level of confidence and respect, visit a couple of these restaurants regularly. You are looking for a restaurant that is in line with your brand. Make sure that the restaurant's noise level and lighting will favour business exchanges.

When making the reservation, make it clear that you will be paying and stress the importance of your meeting. Request a private area, away from the kitchen and the washroom, without distractions.

Call your client the day before to confirm your invitation and review directions or parking options.

Arrive at the restaurant about fifteen minutes ahead of time to meet with the service personnel, the manager or the maître d'hôtel. Review your expectations, including your table, the seating chart and make payment arrangements. If it is possible, pre-pay. This way, the bill will never make it to the table, and it will avoid the usual bill back and forth.

When you are the host of a business meal make sure that you assign seating to reflect the rank and order of your business guests.

In a two-person meal, give your guest the best seat. That place usually has its back to the wall with a great view of the restaurant, the city or the water.

As the host, in a two or three-person meal, you will sit to the left of your client. He/she will then be on your right, which is the traditional place of honour. The third person will sit in front of you.

During a meal with many business associates, you will sit in the middle of the table, in front of your client. You will then assign seating to alternate between your right and your guest's right, then to each other's lefts and back to your rights and so on, according to the pecking order.

When you have an uneven number of guests in your party, it is best to request a round table.

When dining with spouses, you will sit at one end of the table and your spouse at the other end. The spouse of your guest of honour will be seated on your right, and your "Most Important" guest will be on your spouse's right.

Some companies have precise per diems for client entertainment. To stay on budget, pre-choose a couple of meal and wine options. Most restaurants will even personalize menu cards for your party.

Wait for your guests without ordering a drink or eating the bread. When your guest arrives at the table, greet your guest by standing and shaking hands. Show him/her where to sit.

Wait for your guests in the lobby until the reservation time. When your table is ready, go to your table. Let the personnel guide the latecomers to your table.

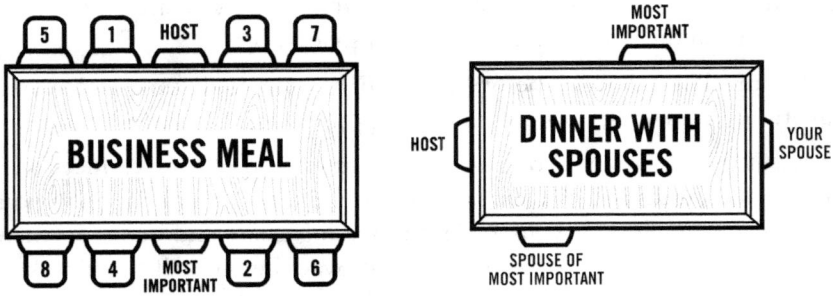

As the host, in a three-person meal, you will sit to the left of your client or most important guest. Guide your guests on the courses and drinks that you will be having. This indicates the rhythm and duration of the meal, as well as your generosity. Choosing a club sandwich and fries with a diet coke versus a four-course meal with paired wines will set different meal time and price expectations.

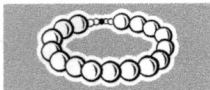

Bread is not an appetizer. It accompanies the meal.

When the waiter comes to take your order, invite your guests to order first.

As the host, you are the person who decides when to talk business. Most North American business meals save the actual business talk for after the main meal, or for coffee time.

If you did not make pre-payment arrangements, discreetly do so after dessert has been ordered. Excuse yourself from the table and go pay the bill.

If the bill does make it to the table take it right away without hesitation and say: "Thank you for accepting my invitation. You are my guest today." Your payment should also include the tip. The typical amount is a minimum of 15% prior to taxes and services. In first class restaurants, where you get extra attention, a generous tip of 20% would be best. This will also help in establishing your client recognition. Never allow a guest to pay for the tip.

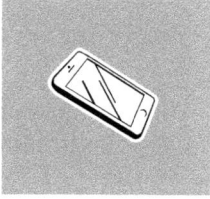

When a guest fights to take the bill away from you, use direct eye contact and in a firm friendly way, say, "I insist. I invited you. You are our guest. You are a good client and the firm is happy to invite you."

As a guest, when the bill makes it to the table and the host does not reach for it, suggest splitting it in two.

| BE A GRACIOUS GUEST

All invitations require a reply, an RSVP (*répondez s'il-vous-plaît*, in French). Whether your invitation is in person, on the telephone or by email, answer in the same manner, as soon as possible, usually within 24 to a maximum of 48 hours.

- If you have food allergies or are on a restricted diet; for religious or medical reasons, and your host does not inquire about them, it then becomes your responsibility to inform him. You could say, "Thank you for the invitation. I would love to come to dinner. I must inform you that I have a severe seafood allergy. I have an anaphylactic reaction to all shellfish."

- If you are on a special, trendy diet, do not inform your host. This would bring undue attention to you. It is only one meal after all and most restaurants offer sufficient selections to accommodate you.

- If you are attending a large banquet or a buffet, there generally is no need to mention allergies or restrictions. Most people can usually find something agreeable and safe to eat, when varieties of foods are offered. To make sure that you are comfortable you can call ahead to inquire about ingredients or discreetly do so when onsite.

By North American standards, there is no such thing as fashionably late, especially for a business meal.

If you are going to be late, inform your dining partner by calling as soon as possible. If you are unable to reach him/her, call the restaurant and ask that your host be informed of your delay. Leave your telephone number, in case your dining partner wants to speak with you prior to your arrival.

If you get there before your host, wait in the lobby. By the reservation time, if your host has not arrived, proceed to your table. It is inappropriate to order a drink or eat the bread before your host's arrival.

When your host shows up, shake hands and exchange greetings. Wait until your host assigns you a seat. If he/she does not show you where to sit; ask "Where would you like me to sit?"Assigned seating allows a host to honour a guest or to accommodate other guests' mobility or dietary restrictions.

> When taking your seat, do so from the right side of the chair. Your left thigh goes in first. Do a torso twist to bring in your knees and the rest of your legs, in. Having this rule avoids guests bumping into each other.

Remember, good posture sends out a message of confidence and power while making you feel good. This also applies to sitting. For the best posture, sit with both feet flat on the ground. Your bum sits at two-thirds to three-quarters of the way in. Your back does not touch the back of the chair.

Looking from above the table, the distances between the table, you and your chair should be one to two hands in the front and in the back.

Do not put your keys, sunglasses, PDAs (Personal Digital Assistant), note-taking material or technology on the table. It all goes in your pocket, purse or under your chair. Business meals, especially the *tête-à-tête*, one-on-ones, are all about face time, the traditional; not the Apple brand kind.

Ladies, your purse goes on the floor or on a purse hook. Placing it on the back of your chair could hinder traffic and even be unsafe; if it falls in the pathway of servers and patrons.

Evening bags and clutches go between your back and the chair or on your lap, under your napkin. It depends on the chair and your bag.

| SOLUTIONS TO MODERN GENDER MANNERS

The contemporary North American workplace is gender neutral; men and women are equal. Therefore, at a business meal a man is not expected to pull out and push in the chair of his female dining companions.

By exception, in recognition of a woman's maturity, today's professional may choose to help an elderly woman. Be aware that today's workplaces also evolving to generation neutral. So observe first how more senior or veteran employees are paying courtesies to the older generations in your organization.

Getting up for a lady, when she excuses herself from the table, is also no longer practiced in business settings. Because our places of business do not discriminate based on gender, a man who gets up for a woman would also get up for a man. Soon the whole table would look like a carousel. For that reason, it is discouraged.

Along the same lines, a man is no longer obligated to open the door for a woman. On the other hand, it is perfectly acceptable, and I strongly encourage you to ask a man or a woman if you can hold the door for them when their hands are full.

As a businesswoman, there may be times when a man displays gender courtesies, you can accept them or simply say: "I am fine thank you" and then proceed to bring in your own chair or open your own door.

Gentlemen, in social situations, these chivalrous behaviours are still generally universally accepted and even appreciated by women, but when in doubt, ask "May I get that door, chair for you?"

| READ THE TABLE WITH LETTERS

> *The world was my oyster but I used the wrong fork.*
>
> −Oscar Wilde

Your place setting is identified with the acronym B-M-W. Your B-read plate is on your left; your M-eal is in the middle, and your W-ine and W-ater glasses are on the right.

Another way of identifying your place setting is by shaping your left and right thumbs along with their indexes to form the letter "b" on the left and the letter "d" on the right. The "b" on the left indicates the b-read plate and the "d" on the right is for d-rinks.

Once you are seated at the table, identify your place setting. Use your utensils from the outside-in. Start with the cutlery to your furthest left and right. Proceed inwards, from one course to the next.

What should I do if someone says grace or a prayer?

As a sign of respect, the appropriate gesture is simply to bow your head. You are not obligated to say a word or make any other action.

What should I do if someone uses my bread plate or drinks from my glass?

Don't make a fuss. Discreetly get the attention of your waiter and ask for a replacement.

Once you have identified your place setting, follow your host's lead for the number of courses and price range. Don't dwell too long to make your selection. It will make you appear indecisive.

PLACE SETTING MAP

When in doubt about which utensil to use, relax, look around, observe your host or someone that appears to know which one to use and follow their lead. As usual, confidence is the key. Breathe, stay calm and carry on.

A. Table napkin
B. Bread plate
C. Bread knife
D. First course or fish fork
E. Dinner fork
F. Salad fork (European service)
G. Soup bowl
H. Dinner plate
I. Charger★

J. Dinner knife
K. Fish knife
L. Soup spoon
M. Water goblet
N. Red wine glass
O. White wine glass
P. Dessert spoon
Q. Dessert fork

★It may remain on the table throughout the meal, or some hosts prefer removing it, at the start of the meal.

Excerpt from *ETIQUETTE: CONFIDENCE & CREDIBILITY*

| YOUR STEMWARE

Your stemware is also placed in its order of service. Your glasses are used from the outside going in. According to the above place setting diagram, you would first be served a glass of white wine to accompany your appetizer. A glass of red wine will then follow with your main course. Your water goblet is last. Of course, you can drink from it at any time. There could also be a flute for the service of champagne during the dessert course, and/or a small sherry glass to begin the meal.

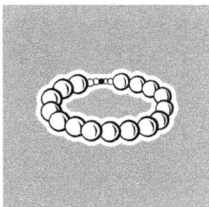

When attending a function where cocktails are served in a separate room, other than where the meal will be served, usually a foyer, leave your cocktail glass in that original room. Do not bring your cocktail glass to the table, even if it is almost full. If you are having a pre-dinner glass of wine, it will not be brought to the table. The reason is simple: the table will be too crowded.

Your dessert utensils may be on the table—as in the place setting diagram, as part of the original table setting, or the service personnel will bring them to you with the dessert course.

When they are on the table, the service personnel may slide them down into position, or you may have to do it.

To bring down your dessert utensils simply follow the direction of their handles. The dessert fork will slide to your left, to occupy the position of your dinner fork. Your dessert spoon will glide to your right, to where your soupspoon was.

Depending on the dessert, your utensils will interchangeably cut or push and the spoon will scoop.

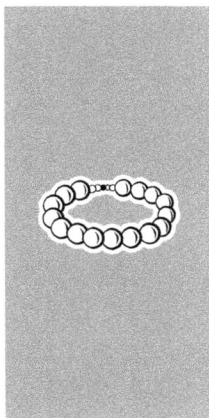

For all business meetings, including dining, place your telephone on silent, or mute mode.

If you are a lifeline for someone, or if you are expecting a business call, inform your host right away of the possible incoming call.

When your call comes in, excuse yourself from the table. Answer and let the caller know that you are excusing yourself from the table. Step away from the table and find a quiet place to converse.

Return to the table as soon as possible. Apologize for the inconvenience and resume dining. No need for personal details, only business-related information should be shared.

Once seated at the table, your hands should be visible at all times. If people do not see them, they are wondering what you are doing with them. Simply rest your forearms on the table for the duration of the meal.

In between courses, elbows are permitted on the table. You may even place your chin on the back of your hands while engaged in conversation.

The *no elbow on the table* taboo goes back to medieval times. Banquet tables were unsecured planks of wood on scaffoldings. The rule was created to avoid silverware, stemware, dishes and food from flying. Imagine what a mess that would make when knights in shining armour would simultaneously rest their elbows on the table!

Today, tables are secured. We keep elbows off the table when plates and food are present. This avoids overcrowding the table and respects all diners' personal spaces.

| SIGNAL SERVICE SILENTLY

At Nascar, you hear "Boogidie, boogidie, boogidie", the flag is waved and the race starts. To indicate the start of a meal, the host or guest of honour, places their napkin on their lap. The other guests follow.

If you are first talking business or making small talk, leave the napkin on the table. When napkins are lifted, they signal to the service personnel that you will soon be placing your order.

Your napkin forms a pouch on top of your legs. Unfold your napkin, flat on your thighs, with the seams showing on top. Take the extremity above your knees and fold it towards your belly, about two-thirds of the way in. This fold gives an impeccable napkin view at all times.

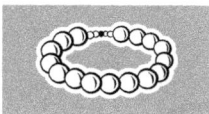

> Your napkin is not a tissue, a washcloth or a bib. Never, ever, use it to blow your nose, absorb your sweat and tuck it in your shirt or pants.

To cleanse soiled fingers: place your hands inside the pouch, palms facing up. Rub your fingers upwards, against the inner top fold of the pouched napkin. The outer edges of the inner top fold are used to absorb droplets of soup or sauce, from the corners of your mouth or on your chin.

At the end of the meal, to indicate your departure from the table; loosely fold your napkin inwards, once or twice, depending upon its size, and place it to the left of your plate.

To signal a temporary absence from the table, fold your napkin once or twice, depending upon its size and place it on the back of your chair. Push your chair in, under the table to allow the service personnel and restaurant patrons to move safely.

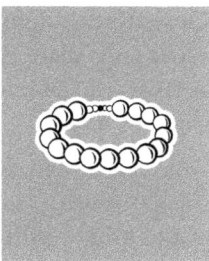

> Etiquette experts do not all agree on the "I will be back" service signal. Some recommend placing the napkin on the seat of your chair. I discourage this practice, because the seat could be made of cloth and the napkin could be greasy. Hence, there is the possibility of staining the seat of the chair and in turn, your behind. Some others recommend placing it to the left. I also disagree with this code as it may be confused with the "I am done" signal.

Your mother, or other adults in your childhood, may have told you to eat everything on your plate. They did so to get you to try out a variety of foods and for economic reasons, so as not to waste food. When eating at the restaurant, you do not control the portion sizes, and you are not there to experiment. You are there to conduct business, to listen and talk. You do not have to eat everything on your plate. That is a personal choice. Therefore, you will not ask other diners why they are not touching certain foods or why they are not finishing their plates.

Every dinner has a rhythm. Stay in tune with it. If you are a slow eater, you may have to speed it up a notch, or if you have a tendency to be the first to finish, slow it down. When hosting, wait for your meal mates to have finished eating to indicate the end of your meal. You do not want to hurry them up.

Utensils silently signal whether we are still eating or have finished your meal.

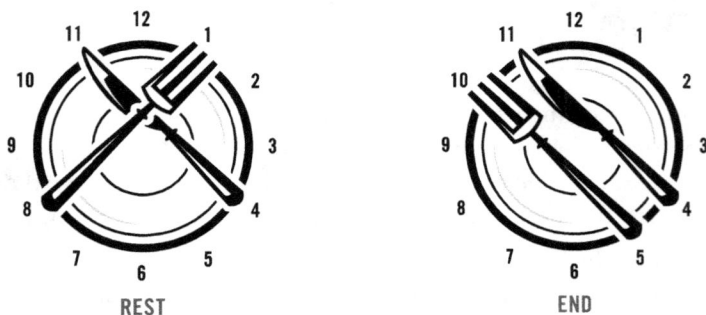

REST

END

Their placement is best demonstrated on an imaginary clock. Picture a traditional numbered clock on your plate.

Forming an inverted "V" signals a pause in your meal. Your knife's blade is inwards, and its handle is between the 4 and the 5. If possible, the fork goes on top of your knife, with its tines down and its handle is closer to the eight of your imaginary clock. At the beginning of the meal, when your plate is pretty full, know that the important element of this code is that, your utensils not touch each other and that their handles for the inverted "V".

Joining your utensils between the 4 and 5 positions on your plate signals the end of your meal. Your knife is at the top with its' blade inwards, to avoid pointing your dining partner with it. Your fork joins the knife inside of your plate.

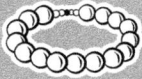

After signalling the end of your meal with your utensils, let the service personnel remove the dishes. Do not push away or stack plates. It is noisy and distracting.

When eating soup, your spoon may be left in a shallow soup bowl to indicate that you are resting. If the bowl is deep, place your soupspoon on its under plate to the right. Once again, the handle is at the 4 position on your imaginary clock. Although this may be confusing, place your spoon in the same position when you are finished eating your soup.

We are not rowing; we are eating. Please bring in your oars.

–Fernande Des Roches, my paternal grandmother

Once you pick up a utensil from the table, it never goes back on the table. Even its handle never touches the tablecloth or the place mat again. You cannot rest your utensil's handle on the table, or on the outside of your plate; even when the tines of your fork or the blade or your knife, are inside of your plate.

When eating several courses with the same utensils, place them on your bread plate in between services.

If you do not have a bread plate, place your fork on the table, tines up, to your left. Slide your knife, blade down, in between two fork tines.

| EATING EUROPEAN VS AMERICAN STYLE

There are two basic eating methods: European and Continental. They are also known as American and Zigzag eating styles. Both methods are appropriate for contemporary business dining.

The American method is only used in North America. The rest of the world uses the Continental method. The Continental technique is preferred for one simple reason: it is less distracting. The Zigzag way, as its' name suggests, involves more utensil manoeuvres and can therefore bring undue attention to one's self.

Whether you are left or right handed, your utensils are held in the same manner for both eating styles. Your knife goes in your cutting hand and your fork in the other.

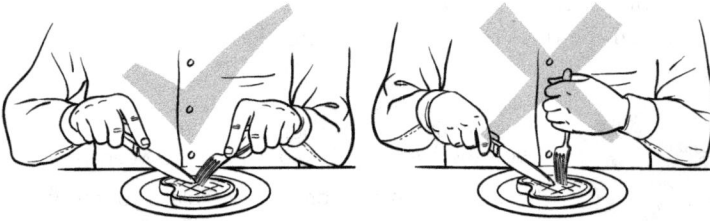

Whether you are eating European or American style, cutting is the same. Your utensils' handles start in the palm of your hands. Your index finger is on top of the back of your fork; Its tines are down to pierce your food. Your knife's blade is placed on the outside of the tines of your fork. You cut one or two pieces at a time. You do not cut your entire meal at once.

Please see the diagram on the left side for the correct way of cutting. The illustration on the right is the inappropriate way of cutting. There is no need to steadily spear your meat with your fist. After all, it is already dead.

For the European eating style, the fork tines are down to convey food to your mouth. Your knife rests in your opposite hand.

For the American eating style, cut your meat, place your knife at the top of your plate. The blade is inwards and should always remain inwards for the duration of the meal. Transfer your fork from your cutting hand to your eating hand. Turn your fork upwards by switching the tines from down to up. Hold your fork as you would a pencil, and not a shovel.

Keep your knife's blade towards you at all times. At the table, in Medieval times, if you had ill intentions and wanted harm done to a fellow knight, you would point your knife's blade in his direction.

Refrain from using your fingers to push food onto your fork. Use your knife or a piece of your dinner roll instead.

Depending on the formality of the meal, its surroundings or your table mates, it could be appropriate to soak up the gravy or sauce juices with a piece of your roll, placed at the end of your fork. Observe first and then decide.

| EATING SOUP

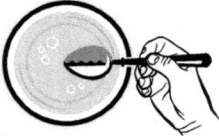

Soup is eaten by holding your spoon, as you hold a pencil. To fill your spoon, skim the top, away from you. Once your spoon is on the other side of your bowl, gently slide it on the back lip of the bowl. This way, soup droppings will fall into your bowl.

The spoon is brought to your mouth and emptied sideways. Please do not slurp. Contrary to when you were a toddler, you do not open wide for the spoon to go in frontwards.

Be aware of your posture. Be careful not to resemble a bobbing, up and down, duckling.

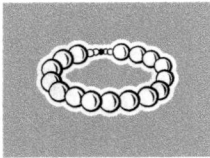

When crackers are served, you do not crush them in their package. You open the wrapper and dispose of it on your bread plate. Break the crackers, above your soup bowl; first in halves and then in quarters. Gently drop them in your soup.

In order to get the last drops of soup, tilt the bowl away from you. Tilting away from you will avoid spillage on your lap.

When there is a handle on the side of the soup bowl, use it to tilt. When two handles are on a soup bowl, it is appropriate to bring it to your mouth to drink its contents. A soup bowl with two handles is usually served for a bouillon, a consommé or a broth.

| EATING BREAD

As stated earlier, bread is not an appetizer. Bread is not to be eaten while waiting for the meal. Bread accompanies the meal. When the first course is served, the person closest to the basket will offer bread to the person to his left. The diner then serves himself and passes the basket to the right.

Circulation around the dinner table is to the right; counter clockwise. Salt and pepper, are a couple. They are always passed together. They are always passed together, even when only one of the seasoning is requested.

When the breadbasket is lined with a napkin, use that napkin to pick up the piece of bread and pass it to your other hand, to deposit it on your bread plate.

If a full loaf is in the basket, use the napkin to secure it to cut a few pieces. Take one piece at a time and leave the remaining pieces for the others.

Do not use the butter directly from the communal dish. Use the serving utensil; knife, tong or fork, to cut or retrieve an individual portion onto your bread plate. If a serving utensil is not present, use your individual butter knife.

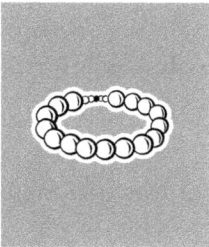

Bread is eaten one small piece at a time. Above your bread plate, tear a bite-size piece of bread, butter it and place it in your mouth. Do not split the bun in halves. Do not spread butter on as you would when preparing a sandwich.

Always cut pieces of bread or food, into mouthfuls of two or three chews. This way, you will always be a few chews away from the conversation.

| SOLUTIONS TO STICKY, CHALLENGING AND FINGER FOODS

The use of fingers to eat some foods may be acceptable at certain times. To eat with your fingers or not depends on the meal's level of formality. In turn, the level of formality is dependent upon the location of the meal but mainly the host's lead.

When choosing foods during a business meal, set yourself up for success. Choose foods that you are comfortable with and that will allow you to stay focused on the agenda.

When your host has made the selection for you, and you are not familiar with the proper way of eating, simply ask your host to demonstrate or observe others around you and imitate them.

As the host, when you notice hesitation on your guest's part, guide them as you eat.

Artichokes

Gently pull each leaf and dip the tender, wider end, in the vinaigrette. Bite the tender part off with your teeth. Leafs are discarded on the side of your plate. Cut out the artichoke's heart with your utensils.

Asparagus

Without sauce on top, you may pick them up by the stalks' end. When served on a side plate with sauce in a bowl, dip them in the sauce.

Bacon

It is best to eat crispy bacon with your fingers. Using your fork and knife could splatter crumbs outside of your plate.

> ### Slippery little suckers.
> –Julia Roberts as Vivian Ward in *Pretty Woman* referring to an escargot that escaped her grip and flew into the hands of a nearby waiter

Finger bowl

When eating shellfish, ribs or corn on the cob with your fingers, restaurants may present you with a finger bowl. Dip and gently shake your fingers in the lukewarm water. Tap your fingers on the side of the bowl before drying them on your napkin.

French fries

When they accompany a sandwich, use your fingers. If they are served with gravy, use your fork.

Lemon or lime squirts

When adding lemon or lime juice, to a meal or drink, shield other diners from your squirts, with your other hand. When done, drop the fruit in your drink or place it on the side of your plate.

Lobster

When it is steamed or boiled, in an informal setting, it may be eaten with your fingers. In a formal setting, use the shellfish fork to retrieve the meat from cracked pieces. At all times, when the lobster is not served in sauce, it is appropriate to suck the meat out of the small legs.

Mussels

When a shellfish fork is not served, use your fingers to remove the first mussel from its shell. The joined emptied shell halves are then used as prongs. By clamping the shells together, extract the meat from the other mussels.

Sushi

Ideally, you should use chopsticks. When they are not present, use your fingers to dip them in soya sauce. Eat them full, in one bite. Taking two bites can be very messy. When eating the sushi in two bites, do not dip a second time in the soya sauce.

Sandwiches; hamburgers, hot dogs, tacos and tea sandwiches

If they are too wide for your mouth cut them in quarters or more manageable, user-friendly sizes. Open face sandwiches should be eaten with a fork and knife.

Shrimps

In a shrimp cocktail or at a buffet, they are eaten from your fingers in one or two bites. When the shells are still on, peel them and discard the shells on your individual plate.

Strawberries

Hold them by the stem and eat them in one or two bites. The leaves are discarded on the side of your plate.

| CHOOSING, TASTING AND TOASTING WITH WINE

CHOOSING ....

As the host of a business meal, you will indicate to your guest(s) if you are serving wine or not. When serving wine, you will also offer the choice of red or white wine.

A host chooses the wine based on the meal choices and his/her company's budget.

> When dining with just one other guest and your guest declines an invitation to an alcoholic beverage, follow your guest and refrain from a pre-dinner cocktail or even wine with dinner.
>
> When your company policy permits you to drink alcohol at a business function, and you choose not to have alcohol, ask your guest if he/she would like an alcoholic beverage while informing him that you will pass. No explanation is necessary.
>
> When your company does not allow you to expense alcohol, and your guest invites you to have a drink that he/she will pay for on a separate bill, the choice is yours. If your company prohibits you from having an alcoholic drink, as their representative, politely decline.

TASTING ....

When the wine arrives on the table, follow these 10 wine tasting guidelines. You are making sure that the wine is not corked—bad, by verifying its' colour, smell and taste.

1. Confirm that what you ordered is exactly what you received. Make sure that the label matches your selection, especially the date. Not doing so could be costly. For example, a Chianti Ruffino Riserva Ducale 1975 or 1957 could have a price difference of about $150.

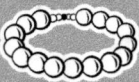

> A damaged wine bottle label has no impact on the quality of the wine. Wine bottles are stored in caves and travel thousands of kilometers to get to your table. A scratch, a small rip or tear, can all be attributed to normal transportation hazards.

2. The server or the sommelier will pour a sampling amount in your glass.

3. At this time, the waiter will give you the cork. You are verifying for mould or extreme dryness. Resist the temptation to play with it and shred it.

4. Hold up your glass by the stem, being careful not to touch its bowl to avoid changing its temperature or soiling the glass. Look at the colour and clarity of your wine. It should be clear of debris and cloudiness. Tiny pieces of cork floating in the wine glass do not mean that the wine is not good. It is more a reflection of your server's lack of wine opening experience.

5. Swirling is optional. It is not necessary. If you are comfortable with it, go for it. It will enhance the scents.

6. Bring the glass up to your nose and sniff the wine's bouquet. It should smell like wine and not vinegar.

7. Take a sip. Here too you are avoiding vinegary tastes. There is no need to rinse and swirl the wine back and forth in your mouth.

8. Inhale the wine, one last time to compare taste and smell.

9. Smile at the waiter and nod in approval, if the wine meets your expectations. If it is corked, a frown or an inverted smile will indicate your disapproval. There is no need to go on with lengthy explanations.

10. When a wine is corked, it is perfectly acceptable, but not necessary, to spit it back into your glass. You may also simply choose to swallow the sip. It is your choice.

As the host, if you are not a wine connoisseur, make sure to talk to the maître d'hôtel. You can discuss wine pairings when you make the reservation, when you arrive early or by calling ahead.

A sommelier friend, with whom I host etiquette dinners, informed me that a good choice is usually the second or third price selection from the bottom.

To drink or not to drink alcohol is a personal choice. One should always feel comfortable declining an invitation for an alcoholic drink.

When choosing not to drink, do not turn your glass upside down. The same rule applies when not drinking tea or coffee; do not turn your cup upside down.

When attending a large banquet or gala dinner and choosing not to drink, let the service personnel pour you one glass of wine. This way, you will be avoiding saying: "No thank you" repeatedly to all the waiters who are trained to offer more wine, or top off an empty glass.

When invited for a business meal, and you are the first to order, err on the side of caution. Order a non-alcoholic beverage. You can always change your mind when your host orders or asks you to join him in an alcoholic beverage.

Tipping the sommelier is not necessary. Restaurants usually have a tipping policy where the wait staff will give a percentage of their tips to the other members of the service personnel, including the sommelier.

TOASTING

The legendary origins of toasting, touching glasses prior to drinking, are associated with medieval poisoning rituals. Conquerors would clink glasses hard enough so that their wines would spill over into their opposite's glass. Suspicious glances would exchange as each party hesitantly took a sip.

The origins of the word toast are attributed to the 17th century Roman practice that made cheaper wines more drinkable. A piece of burnt toast was placed at the bottom of a wine glass to absorb undesirable flavours while decreasing its acidity.

Because we trust one another, we do not clink glasses when toasting. Another reason not to touch glasses when toasting is to avoid breaking glass. This practice could be unsafe and expensive. Fine crystal is delicate and costly.

Although some superstitions discourage toasting with water, these days, it is perfectly acceptable to toast with any beverage.

If your glass is empty, during the toast feign drinking.

A formal business meal with many guests will usually have three toasts:

1. The welcome toast

From a casual gathering to a formal wedding, the first toast is always made by the host. It is stated near the beginning of the event, before the service of the first course of a meal function. The host welcomes, thanks and offers goodwill to all guests. This practice sets the mood for the event. Formal events require that the host stand.

The host taking a sip from his glass concludes the toast. Guests follow.

2. The toast to the guest of honour

This toast is usually made during the first course. The other guests remain seated, unless the host instructs them to stand. The person being toasted always remains seated. The host may remain seated for less formal gatherings.

The toastee simply makes eye contact with the host and guests, smiles, nods then says "Thank you," without raising his glass.

3. A thank you toast from the guest of honour to the host

This toast is usually offered before dessert. Reciprocate in the way the toast was delivered to you; standing or sitting.

When these three toasts are out of the way, other guests may then make a toast.

If midway through the dessert no one has made a toast, a guest may turn to his host to request the privilege of proposing a toast.

| THE MEMORABLE TOAST FORMULA

Prepare your toast in advance. Make it succinct, personable and upbeat. The ideal length is about a minute, with an average of three sentences.

Practice, practice and practice. Do not improvise it.

Do not read from notes.

Ask for people's attention by increasing your voice and saying "Ladies and gentlemen may I please have your attention."

In a crowded room, enlist the help of colleagues, family members or friends. Minutes before you wish to make your toast ask them to go to corners of the room. When you ask for people's attention, request that your helpers direct the guest's attention in your direction.

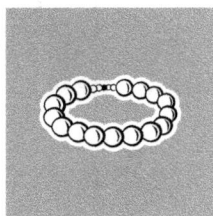

Never ever attract people's attention by:

- Clinking a utensil on a glass
- Whistling
- Standing on a chair
- Yelling

The mechanics of toasting start by holding your glass by its stem. Bring it up between the top of your shoulder and your eyebrows. Look at the guest(s) of honour.

Toasting can also be used to distract when a conversation is getting slippery.

| SOLUTIONS TO STICKY DINING SITUATIONS

The meanders of the human digestive system present business dining situations with unexpected sounds and sometimes dining guests are embarrassed.

Here is a list of such situations and recommendations to keep you in control at the table.

YOU HAVE TO GO TO THE WASHROOM ....

Simply excuse yourself and go. There is no need to inform others of where you are going. The same goes for excusing yourself to place a call. Minimize absences from the table; they are distracting and you can miss a lot of valuable information. Upon your return, do not ask for a recap of the missed conversation.

YOU HAVE A FOREIGN ITEM IN YOUR MOUTH ....

This could be a bone, a piece of gristle or pits. The general rule of thumb is to remove it in the same manner that it went in.

If you are eating a Greek salad, and you placed a pitted olive in your mouth with your fork, you will bring your fork up to your mouth and with your tongue discard the pit onto its tines. You then place it on the side of your plate. To keep your plate visually appealing, camouflage it behind a vegetable or other food item. If the olive is brought to your mouth with your fingers as when eating a couple of them during a cocktail, you can place it in your cupped hand to bring it to your plate or to be thrown out in a paper napkin.

As a courtesy to the service personnel, never place meat gristle in a cloth napkin.

YOU SNEEZE ....

Use your napkin to shield your face from diners. Place your body sideways. Reach for a tissue and dab your nose. Do not blow your nose at the table. If you have to, excuse yourself from the table to go blow your nose.

YOUR BODY MAKES SOUNDS; BURPS OR FARTS ....

Discreetly apologize, "Excuse me."

YOU HAVE THE HICCUPS ....

If they persist, excuse yourself from the table. Request a glass of water from the service personnel and practice your best trick to get rid of them.

YOU SPILL SOMETHING

On the table, try to contain the spillage. You can use your napkin to absorb or stop liquids from spreading. On a guest, offer your napkin, if it is unused. Do not touch the guest, with your napkin or other absorbers, such as a paper towel. Offer to have the garment dry-cleaned. Apologize.

YOU DROP A UTENSIL

In a restaurant, kick it under the table to keep the floor safe for all. Ask for a re-placement utensil. In a private home, bring it to the kitchen and inform your host.

SOMEONE HAS SOMETHING HANGING OR STUCK

Make eye contact with the person who has a dangling or protruding piece or food on their face or elsewhere on their body. Discreetly mirror the location of the piece of food by touching the same location on yourself. When a colleague has a piece of lettuce stuck on their front tooth. Gently glide your tongue between your lip and tooth. Make eye contact with your colleague with raised eyebrows. Nod gently while gliding your tongue. As a last resort, add, "Excuse me" and point to your tooth in the same position as his/hers.

SOMEONE HAS A ZIPPER OPEN OR A BUTTON THAT IS UNDONE

You tell. Ideally, this information is given among members of the same sex. You are a man, and you notice Ms. CEO's top button is undone. Find a female colleague to go inform her. If there is no one, discreetly do it yourself. Unusually in business, this would be one of the rare times, when eye contact would not be necessary. During a meeting, depending upon the formality of the discussion and the people present, you could pass a note. Do it before you start your meal.

A DINING COMPANION TOOK YOUR BREAD PLATE

You have options. Keep calm, don't eat bread and carry on. Or, simply ask for another one. But, the table could become crowded.

YOU WANT TO SHARE YOUR MEAL

Think about how the other guests will perceive it. If you decide that it is appropriate use your bread plate or request a side plate. Make sure not to share with used utensils.

According to etiquette folklore, the original singer of *La vie en rose*, Édith Piaf, was hosted at Buckingham Palace. Towards the end of the meal, elegant waiters with perfect posture carried silver trays of bowls into the state dining room. Serving on the left, the white-gloved service personnel placed a bowl in front of each guest.

Madame Piaf looked down and smelled the aromas of her bowl. It contained a clear liquid and one slice of lemon. She then raised the bowl to her mouth and drank its content. What do you think that Her Majesty did?

Queen Elizabeth II reciprocated by drinking from her finger bowl. All other invitees imitated and carried on. The respectful manner, in which the Queen followed suit, is the essence of being a good host; making all guests feel comfortable without pointing fingers.

SUMMARY

- Prepare for business lunches, especially when you are the host; coordination, seating, conversation, toasts and payment.
- When you make the invitation, you pay for everything.
- The right is the place of honour.
- When you are the host, if possible, pre-pay for the meal and activities.
- Use silent service codes to signal the service personnel without interrupting the meal and conversation.
- Turn off technology during business meals.
- Prepare your toast, even for the simplest of occasions. Keep it short, to thepoint and personal.

Set yourself up for success—avoid difficult foods and make choices that will let you confidently participate in the conversation.

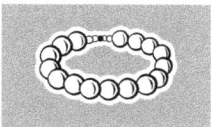

When dining to network, if your plate is full and your guest's plate is empty: you are talking too much. Remember it is not about you; it is about them and building your network.

Conversation is the objective of networking activities. In either case; business dining or networking, you are not invited to eat and drink, because your host thought that you were hungry or thirsty. You are there to build relationships and that is difficult to do, if your mouth is always full. Onto networking, let's empower you with how to successfully connect to build your own safety net.

NETWORK TO INCREASE YOUR NET WORTH

I s in person networking the dreaded "not working" activity for you? Are you uncomfortable walking into a room full of strangers to make the small talk that will, you sincerely hope, lead you to the big talk with the big guy?

If you answered yes, allow me to reassure you; you are not alone. Most of the people that you meet at these meet and greets feel exactly as you do. Introducing oneself, chatting with prospective contacts and exchanging business cards, is not appealing to most people. Just like you, they may be shy and uncomfortable. The next time that you are about to cringe at the thought of attending one of these events, think about the other attendees. Most of them feel just like you.

If you answered no, you are among the few that thrive at networking events. You love meeting people. You probably believe in the Theory of the six degrees of separation[30]. You get excited about making new connections to get to whom you need to know. Chances are that networking is more like "not working" but having fun and meeting people.

> *You can't stay in your corner of the forest waiting for people to come to you. You have to go to them sometimes.*
>
> —Winnie the Pooh

Think of networking as building your own safety net. Picture yourself as a trapeze artist and imagine a net of people supporting you below. Then, reverse the roles. Imagine the people supporting you, individually at the top of the trapeze. It is now your turn to support them. That is the goal of networking; building a mutually supportive net of people. Networking is about helping.

---

[30] http://en.wikipedia.org/wiki/Six_degrees_of_separation

> You may have heard the popular proverb "Tell me who your friends are, and I will tell you who you are." Adopt this philosophy for networking and you get "Your network is your net worth". Your professional contacts make up who you are in the business world.

Networking is about connecting to find mutually beneficial relationships. When thinking about networking, think about whom you can help. To be of assistance to people you must understand what their needs are. That is the basis of networking. That is why we engage in small talk. We converse to figure out what people want, need or are hoping to find. Once you understand what they require, offer it to them or connect them to someone else who can fill that void. Business networking is leveraging your personal and professional contacts to create mutually beneficial business opportunities.

Connecting to help, that is successful networking!

| PREPARE FOR A BUSINESS NETWORKING ACTIVITY

Business networking often occurs during a social activity where you meet and reciprocally gain insight into others. It is all about building relationships by exchanging information, ideas and leads.

When receiving an invitation to a networking activity, evaluate the potential of attending. Too many people do not take the time to appraise if an activity will be beneficial to them. This is crucial. Do so by using the following questions:

- What is the occasion?

- Who is the host?

- Who will be there? Request a list of attendees from the event's organizer, if possible.

- What if I did not attend the event and my competitor did, how would I feel?

- Is there a cause associated with this occasion?

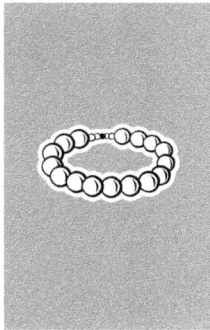

To productively maximize your networking efforts and diminish your travel time, based on the location of the event, seek other meeting opportunities. Geographically regroup your appointments to meet with people before the event, during the event and after the event.

- Invite a client for tea/coffee before the event.
- If possible, invite other colleagues that work in the same area to the event.
- Ask peers to join you for an after event dinner.

When accepting an invitation to a business networking activity, develop a strategy to stay focused. Plan your participation by asking yourself:

- Why am I attending? What made me say yes?

- What am I hoping to accomplish?

- Whom do I want to meet at this event?

DO YOUR HOMEWORK ....

Once you have decided to attend establish your objectives and research the people that you have placed on your radar. Based on your answers to the above "to attend or not to attend" questions, establish your objectives. Research …

I am not telling you to hire a private investigator or to stalk the people on your list. I am simply stating that you should familiarize yourself with the public information that is available about the individuals with whom you want to connect. This includes where they work, what they do, maybe even their hobbies and the causes they support.

On the Internet and in digital networks, it is now easier than ever to obtain this information. You are looking for current projects, initiatives, celebrations and even problems. Peruse LinkedIn, Facebook or simply their company's website to find out what makes them tick and with what they may need help.

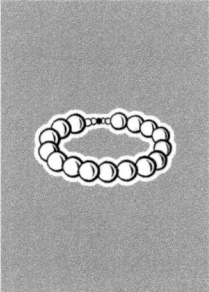

> Another great way of preparing for the event is to volunteer. By volunteering, you will have a purpose, something to talk about, and you will help all that you encounter. All your networking goals will be met by simply giving your time to your network's cause. This is definitely win-win.
>
> As a bonus, you may be privileged to have time, before the official start of the activity, to mingle with, or at the very least be introduced to the coveted guest of honour or speaker.

From your research, you will have topics of conversation that will be of interest to your prospective contacts. Familiarize yourself with them.

EAT BEFORE YOU GO

Just as you do not attend a business meal to eat and drink, you do not attend a cocktail networking event to eat or drink. You do not want to spend happy hour chewing away or downing drinks. You are there to meet and mingle, for business. Stay away from the buffet and the bar. Your mouth will be full, your fingers unavailable to shake hands or hand out a business card and the

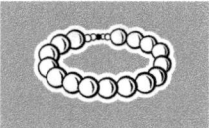

> To make sure that you are ready to connect as soon as you arrive, eat a little before joining the group. Reach for your favourite power snack, such as a granola bar.

bartender, unless you are in the hospitality industry, is not whom you should spend your time get to know better.

DRESS THE PART

Although the event may be held in a bar, you are still there to make professional contacts. What you wear should reflect who you are in the business world.

ARRIVE WITH YOUR FOCUS IN MIND ....

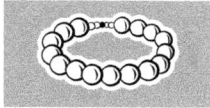

> Before you get into networking mode, silence your telephone. Face-to-face, not screen time, is the way to build a relationship.

From the moment that you step out of your car, the taxi, the train, the plane, the metro or the bus, open the door to the building or get in the elevator, you may be in contact with others that are also attending the same event as you.

As soon as you are on-site and for the duration of the event, until you have left the building, make sure that all your actions and your words, even the ones

> You are stuck in a line-up. Count your blessings! You have just been presented with two networking opportunities: one in front of you and one behind you.
>
> You also have the bonus that there will be a smooth exit, if you need it, to end your conversation; when you get in the front of the queue. That will be your natural good-bye cue. If you have made a good connection, you can wait for the person or exchange information to meet at a later time.

| WALK IN, POSE AND SCOUT

Before you make your entrance go to the washroom and practice your power pose.

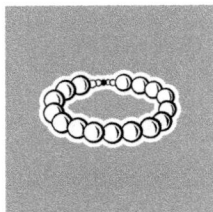

> As you have read, in *CONTROL YOUR FIRST IMPRESSION,* all we have are seven seconds to make a positive first impression. With this knowledge in mind, be aware of your first seven steps, your first seven words and the top seven inches of your face. This checklist of sevens is what others will be looking at to make their connect or not decision.

As you enter, do not head to the bar or for the nibbles. I repeat, do not go on a quest for food and beverage. Networking is about connecting, not eating and drinking.

Think about the great entrances that you have witnessed through the years. Think of world leaders and stars going through thresholds. Think back to the cool kids that entered the school's cafeteria. All the students turned around, whether they knew them or not. All of these people walk in happy and believe that the other attendees are happy to see them. They have presence. They own the room.

Now that your cortisol is down and your testosterone is up, thanks to your two-minutes of power posing, here's how to walk in and own the room. Do a mental check for confidence and credibility. Walk through the door, shoulders back, head up straight, look ahead and step to the right. Stop. (Really, take a brief pause.) Madonna says "Vogue", I say, "Pose". Look around and scout the horizon for the whereabouts of the guests whom you have pre-identified on your list of contacts. Simultaneously, you are in search of a group that you can join. Observe the body language of the other attendees to choose a trio that seems open to a newcomer joining in.

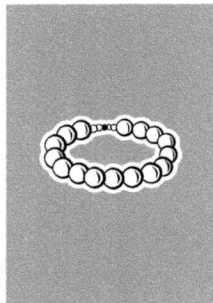

> The Protocol School of Washington's President and Owner, Ms. Pamela Eyring beautifully demonstrated this entrance; through the door, to the right and pose, to me, and my distinguished international colleagues. It was the first day of our *Corporate Etiquette and International Protocol Consultant* course.
>
> When Pamela walks into a room, people know that she is someone they should meet. Ms. Eyring is a tall, beautiful woman who inspires many, including me, with her poise and confidence.

Through the door, to the right and pose, has the added benefit of having you be seen by other guests. As you are looking at the other guests, they are wondering who you are. Additionally, the attendees that know you will be happy to recognize you and will be quick to invite you over.

When looking to introduce yourself to a small group, you are ideally in search of a group of three or five, that is having a good time. Look for people that seem relaxed and open.

Another option is to stay close to the door and play host for a moment. Wait for the next person and introduce yourself. You have just made a new connection.

If you prefer the more casual approach, this one may be for you. Walk around the room at a leisurely but confident pace, with open body language. Be ready to accept eye contact with someone who may also be looking for someone new with whom to connect. When you have that meeting glance, stop. Ask permission to join. You are on your way to making a new connection. You will be surprised at how many people will be glad, even relieved, that you were there at the right moment. You could very well be saving someone from a clingy new contact.

MEET AND GREET ....

When approaching a group or a person, always ask if you can join in. Introduce yourself with your full name.

It is also a good idea to add how you are associated to the event or the guest of honour. This is a perfect conversation starter.

> In business, always use your first and last names. Only using your first name makes you half as powerful. By adding your last name, you are making yourself distinct, easier to identify. Throw in your title and the company that you work for and you are memorable, one of a kind.

Complete your self-introduction by shaking hands with each person, when in a group of four or less. For groups of five and more it may simply be best to nod your head. Based on your observations of the group's body language, use your judgment and adapt to the incoming greetings. Go with the flow of the group.

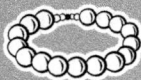

The most popular question for my *Networking to Increase your Net Worth* training activity is "What are your favourite tips for remembering names?" Here they are:

- Repeat, repeat and repeat but be careful not to overdo it. You know what I mean. It will get on the other person's nerves.

- Categorize it with the others that have that same first name.

- Associate it with an object, an image or make it rhyme with a word "Anna, banana."

- Spell it out in your mind. It is said that Franklin D. Roosevelt could remember the first names of most people he encountered. He did so by imaginatively writing peoples' names on their foreheads, as they spoke.

- When participating in a meeting, write it down in your notebook.

- If you have another tip for remembering names, I would love to read about it. Please email me at julie@etiquettejulie.com.

| SOLUTIONS TO STICKY NAME SITUATIONS

What should you do if you have an original name or one that is difficult to pronounce?

Do the others a favour. Help your new contacts by slowly repeating your name after first stating it. You can also give pronunciation hints by rhyming it with a common word or making word associations. If your name is extra long, in my experience, a successful strategy is to adopt a diminutive and introduce yourself with it.

On the other side, what should you do if you did not get the person's name?

This one is a lot simpler than you may think. Simply say something like "I want to make sure that I pronounce your name correctly, could you please repeat it for me?" Then repeat it and validate. "Is this correct?"

What should you do if you know that you know that person, but that you have forgotten their name?

Simply admit it by stating "Hi. It is nice to see you again. I remember you from _____ (fill in the blank with as many details as possible). Please forgive me you are very familiar to me, but my memory is having one of those days. Please refresh my memory with your name. Help me place you." "You're good! Thank you for remembering my name. Please refresh my memory. It's been one of those days." You could also take the lead and reintroduce yourself by beginning with a handshake "Hi, Julie Blais Comeau, Etiquette Julie. It is nice to see you again. It has been a long time since the *Backpack to Briefcase* training day. How are you?" Inevitably, the other person shakes your hand and completes the meet and greet scenario. No matter how you say it, keep it brief. There is no need to publicly belittle yourself. Forgetting names happens to all of us.

Never shorten someone's name without his or her consent. I am always surprised when someone, other than a loved one, calls me Jewels. Richard may not like being Dick. On the flip side, Elizabeth may prefer being Liz. Listen well to self–introductions and respect the stated names.

This also applies to email. The person's signature will give you the clue as to how you should refer to them. When first and last name are present, use the honorific Mr. or Ms. and last name.

Never, ever use terms of endearment in a work setting. "Sweetie", "Honey", "Doll" and even "Girls" can be viewed as sexist.

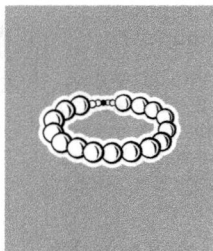

> As you conduct business globally, you will encounter a variety of greetings, including the hug, the air-kiss, the bow and even the Namaste (the non-contact Indian salutation of joined palms with fingers upward, accompanied by a slight head bow). As a guest, you should adapt to your host's customs. Prepare ahead by doing your research. When in doubt at destination, find out from your host.

When you are the host of the event set the mood by welcoming attendees and introducing yourself to them as they arrive. For as long as I can remember, for all of my training activities, I greet participants as they enter the room. I go up to each newcomer, smile, put out my hand and say "Hi, I'm Julie Blais Comeau. I'll be your presenter today. Welcome. Please help yourself to morning treats. (I walk over with them. If many participants are arriving at the same time I show them where to go with the palm of my hand.) Enjoy your day." I do this to build rapport with my audience. It works. On more than one occasion, when reviewing the evaluations for the training activity, participants have commented on how this small introduction set the tone for the training and demonstrated business etiquette in action. It meets their expectations from the get-go.

> The origin of the air-kiss (la bise) is related to physical well-being. French family members, greeting each other, could detect digestive or health problems based on the smell from the body or the breath.

INTRODUCE TO POSITION THE PLAYERS ....

When attending a networking event with colleagues, a spouse or family members, always introduce him/her/them to those you meet. The goal of making introductions is to position the players in the pecking order and to give some information so that the newly introduced can have a conversation.

I know, you may be feeling a little bit of anxiety about screwing this one up. Relax; making introductions is not as complicated as it once was.

The contemporary and easy formula for making introductions always starts with stating the name of the Most Important person. Most Important is the person you want to honour or flatter.

At the top of the pyramid of business introductions is the client. It then follows to the members of the organization based on hierarchy and precedence.

If you are not sure which title is more elevated on a company's organizational chart, do not fret over it. As the Nike motto goes, "Just do it". For the next time, find out afterwards from a trusted source, like an administrative assistant.

Introductions are made so no one is left standing wondering who is who, or on the flip side having to wait for a lull in the conversation to jump in and introduce one-self.

Remember, business is gender neutral so there will be no preference for women over men.

| SIX-STEP INTRODUCTIONS FORMULA

The formula depends on the level of formality within your relationships. It uses titles and names according to the company's culture and its hierarchy.

1. To keep things simple and untangled, start all your introductions by stating the name of the Most Important person. According to your regular interactions with this person, use his/her official title, Mr./Ms. or first name plus, in all cases, his/her last name.

2. Add one of the following phrases – which are stated from most to least formal: "May I introduce____" "I would like you to meet___" "This is___"

3. Fill in the ___ with the official title of the person who is being introduced, Mr./Ms. or first name plus, in all cases, his/her last name and the company name.

4. Then, turn to the person who is being introduced (who is not the Most Important person) and use your usual way of calling him/her. State your usual way of calling the Most Important person and add his/her title and company.

5. In a more formal setting it could sound like this:
"Ms. Client, may I introduce our leader, Mr. CEO of Company Name." You then turn to your leader "Mr. CEO, I'd like you to meet Ms. Client. She is the Title for Company Name."

6. Complete the introductions by giving both parties something they can chat about, something they may have in common, like: they are from the same town; they are fans of the same sports team or enjoy the same leisure activities. "Monica, you and David have both visited the Champagne region last year. I'm sure that you have great stories to share."

When introducing a group of people, introduce them in order, according to rank by starting with the highest. As per the guidelines in the above Introductions Formula use first and last names along with titles and company names.

At a networking event, when you are the one who will make the introductions, welcome a newcomer to your group by naming the group members first. Then present the newcomer with his full name, title and company. Let the people in the group to detail their info as they shake hands with the new one. In a casual setting, it could sound like this:

"Maryse, J-F, Philippe and Florence, I'd like you to meet Rick King, Chief Adventure Officer for Fun Strategies."

| ADJUST YOUR ELEVATOR PITCH

> **Be yourself. Everyone else is taken.**
>
> —Oscar Wilde

The elevator pitch is what you do, how you do it and why you do it. In just a few sentences, even your grandma should understand your purpose in the business world. Succinctly, and to the point, in the time that it takes for an elevator ride (hence its name), a dream client should be excited about your product or service. Your elevator pitch goal is for that prospect to say "How exciting! I need you."

> The scene takes place in a salon, as I am getting a manicure, before the University of Ottawa Alumni Association 10th annual Etiquette Dinner.
>
> I am sitting at the nail station, reviewing my notes, with both hands out on the manicurist's table. She made eye contact and asked:
>
> "What do you do?"
>
> "I am an etiquette expert."
>
> "Ah…" she replied and went back to applying pink nail polish to my perfectly manicured nails.
>
> A few minutes later she looked back up at me:
>
> "So you know a lot about tickets eh? Interesting. Tickets… as in parking tickets, right?"
>
> "Well, if I do my job and teach people well, police officers won't have to hand them out anymore."
>
> I answered while smiling.

A good elevator pitch will describe how you can help any prospect. To be perfect, an effective elevator pitch needs to be personalized, planned, and practiced.

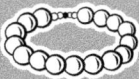

> To efficiently present your elevator pitch, get the other person to speak first. Listen well to be able to engage that person.

Engage the other person in conversation with the follow conversation openers:

- What is a typical day like for you?
- What has been your proudest accomplishment?
- What's it like to be a _____?
- What are some of your challenges?

Remember to listen to all of the messages; yes the verbal but also the visual and the vocal clues. Listen and look. You will soon find out what makes the other person tick, what kind of challenges they have and more importantly how you can help.

COURTESY OF ETIQUETTEJULIE.COM

ELEVATOR PITCH AID

What?

This is your tag line. With just a few words paint a story of what you do with action words.

____

____

____

____

____

How?

Think of qualifiers that describe your services or your product. Write as many as you can think of and circle your three favourites.

____

____

____

____

____

Why?

What are the benefits of doing business with you and your company? How are you different from the competition? Answer these questions from your prospect's perspective "What is in it for me?" Try to input numbers, statistics, percentages and dollars that positively support your results.

____

____

____

____

____

Now put it all together in two to three sentences. Play with it. Say it aloud. It should flow and have rhythm. Practice at every opportunity you get, including social events like your neighbour's annual BBQ or when meeting hockey parents.

____

____

____

____

____

Excerpt from ***ETIQUETTE: CONFIDENCE & CREDIBILITY***

For me, it sounds something like this, "I am a business etiquette expert, *Sticky Situations* blogger and author. I teach people how to broadcast positively, from the boardroom to the banquet. My clients are university students to rocket scientists." This usually prompts a smile and question "Scientist, really? What does etiquette have to do with science?" I then tailor my answer, based on what the person does, to include one of my training topics. "Well even a rocket scientist will need to know which fork to use at dinner, or how to dress, for an awards gala." Later in the conversation, I add my numbers: more than 50 satisfied clients, 500 presentations to date and 5000 empowered participants.

Depending on whom I am speaking with, I will adapt my elevator pitch. Sometimes I might even use "I'm in the nice business. I correct people and stop them from embarrassing themselves. But don't worry I'm not on duty today."

Either way your goal is to open up the communication to lead into a conversation, not a monologue.

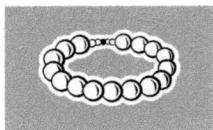

> Remember an elevator pitch is not one size fits all; keep it fresh for the person, the occasion, or the moment. Wait until you have some information on the person to adapt it to their needs.

Do not rush your elevator pitch to get it over with. Make small talk, listen and when asked be ready to explain what you do in tangible advantages for the new person that will now be a part of your professional network.

An effective way of presenting what you do differently is to start with some-thing like, "You know how—*insert a problem or how your competition does what you do?* Well I—*insert what you do and how.*" For example "You know how the people that usually display etiquette knowledge seem to be snobs and are usually passés? Well, I teach modern manners in a way that is relevant with concrete tips for today's lifestyle."

| THE SMALL TALK THAT LEADS TO THE BIG TALK WITH THE BIG GUY

When thinking about networking, most rookies' biggest concern is "What am I going to talk about?" That is the number-one networking mistake. When attending a networking event, it is not about you; it is about them, the other people that you will meet.

Being a good networker is a lot more about listening than talking.

> We have two ears and one mouth. It is recommended that we converse with this 2:1 ratio in mind.

Listening also includes paraphrasing, summarizing and asking questions. Your body language should reflect that you are paying attention. Make eye contact. Nod. Stay clear of one-word answers, as they have a tendency to end the conversation abruptly. Good ways of keeping the conversation going include:

- Uh-huh…
- Right, I understand; I get it.
- That is interesting.
- I never thought about it that way.
- Really? Tell me more.

When conversing, avoid looking over the person's shoulder or scouting the landscape of the room to seek better or more interesting speaking opportunities. Nobody likes that feeling of second best while waiting for someone better. Show genuine interest. This may be done by asking open-ended– questions that can be expanded on and that require more than one word answers, but also by contributing to the conversation.

> *A conversation is a dialogue, not a monologue. That is why there are so few good conversations: due to scarcity, two intelligent talkers seldom meet.*
>
> –Truman Capote

You are at a networking event to funnel information. When meeting people in person, you usually start large and wide. As your relationship evolves, your conversations become narrower, more targeted and personal. This allows you to identify clearly how you, or your network, may be able to help the other person.

Small talk intimidates many business professionals. Many people call it trivial. The fact remains that polite, informal discourses, help to establish rapport with colleagues, clients and even competitors.

Do your homework before attending the event. Find out about the organization that is hosting the event, their members, the guest of honour and invited guests. Make a list of those to whom you can offer assistance.

Have a couple of safe conversation topics that include recognizing recent achievements or honours and current or upcoming events. Once again, in our digital era, you are only a few clicks away from this valuable information. You can usually get interesting conversation topics just by perusing the websites of the event host or other attendees.

Appropriate conversation topics include:

• What is happening in the world, in your country or city

• Current as well as upcoming cultural, sporting or entertainment events

• Company or employee accomplishments

The most obvious conversation starter is asking about the other person's connection to the event or guest of honour. "How are you connected with this organization?" "How do you know our guest of honour?" "How long have you been a fan of this author?"

You can also ask a question or make a comment about the location. "It is my first visit since the renovations. They did a great job! And yourself, had you been here before the renovations?"

Giving a sincere compliment also works. "What a great jacket that is!"

Answering the customary "How are you?" with "Great, I just _____ (fill in the blank with one of your recent successes or exciting upcoming project)" is perfect to highlight one of your accomplishments while setting the conversation up for your elevator pitch.

As you know, politics, religion, money and sexual matters are slippery subjects. I used to call these inappropriate subjects. I now believe that all of them, except sexual matters, can be used in conversation if they do not involve personal opinions. Limit discussions to generalities and observations and you will be safe from awkwardness and embarrassment. Relate facts rather than individual values.

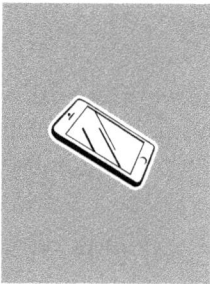

When you are in conversation with someone who has opposing views to yours, and you are equally passionate about your beliefs, your best option is to agree to disagree.

"Louis, you have as much passion about your hockey team, as I do about mine. I know that we can both go on for hours about which team is the best. Let's agree to disagree and just focus on Nicole's promotion celebration."

D.I.N.E. is an acronym that was created by a dear colleague, Sue Jacques. It is designed to remind us of inappropriate topics of conversation, especially at the table. Do not talk about anything that is Disgusting, Insulting, Negative and Emotional.

To find out how to get out of sticky conversation situations read this blog on my website *Answering Nosy Questions*[31]

A good conversation should go back and forth. Both parties are responsible and take turns listening, questioning and sharing. Like dancing or a Ping-Pong match, conversation should be well balanced with active participation by both parties. Share stories, relate to the people you talk with.

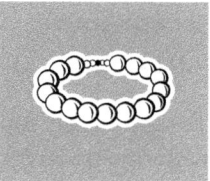

Talk to everyone, not just the people in the room. Start with the door person; this will get you in the mood. Talk to the people in front or behind you when you are waiting in line. When you serve yourself a cup of coffee, do so for the next person too. That is a great conversation opener.

---

[31] http://www.etiquettejulie.com/?q=story/answering-nosy-question

| DO NOT DEAL OR FOLD BUSINESS CARDS

Once upon a time, getting someone's business card was a networking goal in itself. The contact information provided by the three and a half by two-inch card opened up the communication channels with a prized prospect. You had the info to call, write or send a package.

Since the arrival of email, such privileged information is now most often shared during an email cold call.

Always carry business cards with you. You never know whom you will meet and who will need you. Prospective clients are everywhere, not just at business events. When attending a social event offer your card and make arrangements to have the business talk at a more appropriate time. During a business meal, exchange cards after the meal.

Business cards should be impeccable and up to date. Your business card is a snap shot of you, on paper. It represents you. Just as you would not show up in a wrinkled suit, do not keep crinkly business cards.

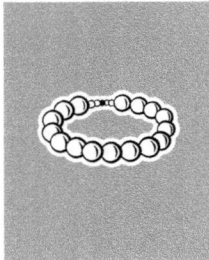

The person with the most authority is the person that asks for the other's card.

The person of lesser authority may offer the person of higher authority his/her card. However, the person of lesser authority may not ask for the business card of the person of higher authority.

You hand out your business card when someone asks for it.

Do not be a black jack dealer. Distributing your cards to all in sight makes you look like a croupier handing out junk mail. Do not hand them out, or accept them, without having exchanged information with the person first. When you get back to your office your should be able to put a face to the card.

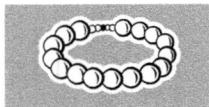

Remember, networking is not about collecting business cards. It is about building relationships, and that takes time.

To keep your cards in mint condition, it is best to keep them in a cardholder. The ideal case has two sides. This type makes it easy for you to keep the cards you receive separate from yours. When attending a networking event, it is appropriate to keep cards in my blazer's right-side pocket. This will make for a quick presentation of your card without having to find your case and open it up. I personally like to keep them in my pant's right side pocket.

Present your business card with your right hand or with both hands. When receiving a card, reciprocate the way in which it was offered to you.

Make eye contact and smile throughout the exchange.

It is considered rude to put the card away immediately. Look at it. Look at the person. Make the mental connection to your memory. Make a comment about it: the logo, the interesting position title or even ask for clarification on the pronunciation of the person's name.

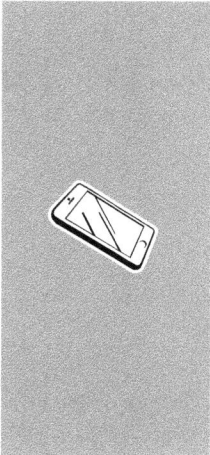

Cultural notes

- In some Asian cultures, writing on a business card is like writing on someone's face. In the same cultures, putting a card in your back pocket and then sitting on it is like sitting on someone's face. If you need to write a note, do it on another piece of paper.

- In some cultures, the left hand is considered soiled and unclean. You should therefore, never present a business card with your left hand. If you do, it could be considered as an insult.

- When traveling abroad it is a nice gesture to have a bilingual card: English on one side and the language of your host on the other side. Present your card with the recipient's language side up.

When you are back in your office, make sure to add the cards' information to your contact list. Asking for another card would be a faux pas.

Always follow up on contacts with whom you have exchanged cards. Sending an email with an interesting article, free information or coupons for your services or product, are all good ways of staying in touch.

| KNOW WHEN AND HOW TO GO

A cocktail networking event is about moving around and meeting people, mixing and mingling. The usual amount of time spent with one person varies from the polite ten minutes to the "Wow, I just made a great connection!" of twenty minutes. On average, you meet about five new business contacts per activity.

To exit a conversation that is boring, dragging on, or when the other person does not seem to have any interest in moving on, plan it, remain calm and simply excuse yourself, during the next pause.

First, wait for a lull in the conversation. Make eye contact, smile and say something like "It was great meeting you. I hope that _____ (fill in the blank). Good luck." Complete your departure by shaking hands and go. That is it! You could add something like "I see my boss over there, and I should go over and say hello." Only use this tactic truthfully.

> Be careful of mentioning where you are going. Some people will take this as an invitation to follow you to the bar, the buffet or even to freshen up in the bathroom. They may say, "Me too" and then will accompany you. You were just caught!

Another option is to introduce this person to another person in your network. You stay a bit with both and then move on, away from the pair. You may have just made a perfect match.

> One of business' stickiest situations is gossip. Within the word, you can find what to do about it 'Go'. Simply put, do not take part in it. We've all done it, but that does not make it acceptable. We all have stuff worth gossiping about. So, do onto others, as you would like done unto you. Don't gossip.
>
> If you stay without saying anything, people will assume that you are agreeing with what is being said.
>
> You could simply excuse yourself and go, without making a scene, rolling your eyes or sighing. You could even smile and say: "Oh my! I have way too much to fix in myself, to talk about others. Please excuse me."

If you want to follow up with the person that you just met, offer your card, "May I offer you my card?" and inform him of how and when you will be following up.

When leaving the event, make sure to thank those responsible for the event. In the next chapter, I will share an easy five-step process for writing thank-you notes.

| THE PARTY TRICK FOR A SHAKE-READY HAND

Social networking, the old-fashioned way, in person, does not allow you to multi-task much. You must, at all times, keep your right hand clean, slip free, and ready to shake hands or hand out a business card.

Keep your purse and/or your drink in your left hand.

Your name badge goes on your right.

When face-to-face, the other person will be able to read your name by following his hand to yours and up, glance up, to read from left to right. The left side is reserved for objects of the heart and honor: a boutonnière, a corsage, medals or your professional alliance

If you must eat a little, drink a little and shake a little, here is the way to do it while keeping everything balanced.

1. Place your napkin over your left pinkie.

2. Add your plate between your middle and ring fingers.

3. Your glass is secured between your middle finger, index and thumb.

4. Practice, practice and practice in the comfort of your own home.

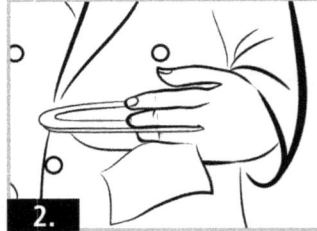

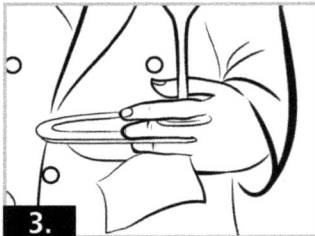

| FOLLOW UP GRACIOUSLY

After the Power Breakfast, the Wine and Cheese or the Chamber of Commerce's luncheon, you are back in your office with a fresh stack of business cards.

> If you have a newsletter, do not add a new contact without their consent. It is illegal. You can ask them about it in a follow-up email or when inviting them to connect on LinkedIn.

Reconnecting after a first encounter is a very powerful way of keeping the connection alive. It sends the message that you are proactive. If you promised to do or send something, do so as soon as possible. This will demonstrate that you have integrity.

Before you take out your pen and paper, or start to type, prioritize and qualify your contacts. You should interact with the most interesting people within a couple of days. The more distant connections can wait for up to three weeks.

Remember, networking is not about collecting business cards and there is no pre-set generic formula. It is about building relationships. Take the time to customize your follow-up.

There are different ways of following up. The important thing is to make it relevant to your conversation and how you may help the person. Some of my favourites are:

• Send a personalized thank-you note to those you enjoyed meeting.

> Include the organizers, the hosts and the event's speaker in your list of handwritten thank you notes. Few people take the time to recognize those whom made connections possible.

• Invite to connect on social digital networks; start with a LinkedIn connection and then follow them on Twitter or like them on Facebook or even comment on their blog. (Words of caution: Do not be overzealous by simultaneously bombarding them.)

• Send an article that could be of interest.

• Invite for a meeting, a business meal, and a sporting or cultural event.

• Connect the person with someone else that may be of value to him or her.

- Invite to attend another networking activity within their areas of interest.
- Recommend a book, a movie, even a store or a professional service provider.
- Send congratulatory notes when they make the news.
- Send a holiday card or birthday card.

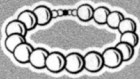

Because someone does not write, call, or follow up with you does not mean that he/she is not interested. Continue the conversation or share information up to three times and then let it go.

NETWORKING AID

Networking activity _____

Date _____ Time _____ Location_____

Contact person _____

Telephone number _____ Email _____

Why am I attending? State your objectives.

_____
_____
_____
_____
_____

Who do I want to meet? Why? What do I know about them?

_____
_____
_____
_____
_____

My elevator pitch

_____
_____
_____
_____
_____

Who I met	Follow Up	Date

Excerpt from *ETIQUETTE: CONFIDENCE & CREDIBILITY*

SUMMARY

- Prepare for all networking activities.
- Walk in, pose and scout.
- Adjust your elevator pitch. It depends upon the person, the event and the evolution of your position.
- Take good care of your business cards. They are an extension of you.
- Follow up with a purpose.

As you now know, successful networking is made up of mutually beneficial relationships. In essence, your network is you. Think of every person in your network as a dot, a pixel. Combine all of the pixels together and you get a picture of: you.

To continue to grow your network positively, remember to acknowledge and thank your contacts for services rendered, introductions made or successful connections. Showing gratitude is much more than saying thank you and can be done in a variety of ways as will be detailed in the next chapter.

THANK TO BE REMEMBERED

n Guideline #6—*CONTRIBUTE TO CIVILITY @ WORK*, we reviewed the power of the magic words to create harmony in your place of work. The positive influence of "Thank you" extends well beyond the spoken words. As a businessperson, to recognize and appreciate, you can spread gratitude by writing notes and offering gifts.

The occasions are numerous:

- A colleague helped you out
- A network connection referred you a client
- A boss gave you extra time to take care of a personal matter
- A subordinate went beyond the call of duty
- A supplier did you a favour
- After a business meal, a sporting or cultural event, an interview, a conference, a visit or the signing of a new contract
- When you receive a gift, etc.

"Who has recently received a thank-you note, in a business context?".

Although considered archaic by many, in my professional opinion, the thank-you note is the most cost-effective and underutilized business practice of our modern era.

I conclude most of my presentations by spreading the word about this easy goodwill written memento. I start this module of my presentation by asking who has recently received a thank-you note, in a business context. A few hands usually go up. I follow up with a couple more questions "Email or paper?" and "What did you do with it?"

The majority of people that receive email thank-you notes; read them, feel good, appreciate the gesture and delete them. Yes, a small number of people do print and post them in their office, well in sight.

The ones that receive a handwritten thank-you note or card; read them, feel good, appreciate the gesture, place them on their desk for a while, post them on their board for another little while and store them as a keepsake in a box or file. Some photocopy them for their superiors and HR.

For your email thank yous, forward them to your superior and to all that collaborated with you.

Typing a thank-you note on your computer is acceptable, but taking out a pen and paper is better.

Think of the time that the person took to organize the meeting, to purchase the gift or to do you a favour and invest the time to write by hand.

Whatever one does with a paper thank-you note, its longevity is a lot longer than that of the verbal or virtual version. There is also the delightful surprise of a coloured envelope in a stack of business correspondence. Moreover, let us not forget, the growing anticipation as the person opens the envelope. A thank-you note is a nice thing.

Gratitude should be expressed as soon as possible. A written thank you should leave your desk within 24 to 48 hours after the event, the gift or the action that you appreciated and wish to recognize.

It is never too late to send a thank-you note, but it does get harder as time goes by. You do not want to add an apology with your thank you. Do not procrastinate, just do it! Keep reading to find out how.

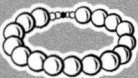

> When deciding on whether to send a paper thank you, an email thank you or even a text thank you note consider: the occasion, your relationship with the person and the timeline.

Thank-you notes leave a lasting impression.

COURTESY OF ETIQUETTEJULIE.COM
THANK-YOU NOTE TEMPLATE

It all starts with your writing tools. Choose a black or blue ink pen.

Just like you have an inventory of pencils, file folders and sticky notes; keep thank-you notes and cards on hand.

Purchase high-quality stationery that reflects your company and its values. It could be made by a local artist or be bought from a charity that you support. Some employers also give employees high quality note cards with company logos. Those must be small and ideally on the back.

When I began writing thank-you notes, I found myself writing the pair of gratitude words—thank you, at least twice, more than likely three times, in just a few sentences, so I developed an easy five-step process.

1. Greet the giver/coordinator of the event.
   Use "dear" or "the person's first name or title" or "last name", depending upon your relationship and the circumstances.

2. Express your gratitude.
   Start with "How wonderful, delightful or nice ___" or "What a beautiful, kind or generous ___" or "I was honoured ___" according to your personality and the gift, the service or the wishes.

3. Name the specifics, make it personal.
   Gift usage, benefits or feelings brought on by what you received.

4. Make a reference to the person and/or the future.
   Write about your relationship to that person, what they mean to you and refer to the possibility of a connection soon.

5. Conclude with gratitude and regards.

Thank-you notes may also be sent through inter-office mail. They can be left on a colleague's desk, at the end or start of the day, or even during a break. It will create impromptu kindness. The sight of it is sure to bring an instantaneous smile to its recipient and it sends out good will vibes throughout the entire office.

Excerpt from *ETIQUETTE: CONFIDENCE & CREDIBILITY*

| WRITING A THANK-YOU NOTE

I have often heard professionals recount their memories of this caring gesture with sincere appreciation. Some even take them out and reread them, when they are having a bad day.

What is the thank-you note's value? Priceless.

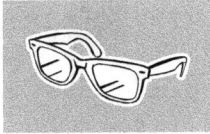

> Watch this inspiring Hannah Bencher video: Love letters to strangers[32] for the power of receiving an impromptu kindness note. It all started with a young lady's therapy for keeping the depression demons away.

I believe that the same good feelings can be generated through thank-you notes. Spread the gratitude, it will come back ten-fold.

---

[32] http://www.ted.com/talks/hannah_brencher_love_letters_to_strangers.html

| OFFERING THE PERFECT GIFT

The famous saying "It is not the gift that counts but the thought" is true, especially in business. Nevertheless, gift giving can be a sticky situation.

To give or not to give? To whom? What? What is the connection with me, my services or products, and the company that I represent? These are all valid questions, and you must think more than twice before settling on your gift choice.

In 2009, when British Prime Minister Gordon Brown visited President Barack Obama, in the United States, he bore three gifts. The first was a framed official paper for the commissioned HMS Resolute; the ship from which timber was used to make the oval office's Resolute desk. Secondly, he had a penholder, crafted from its anti-slave sister ship, the Victorian HMS Gannet. Lastly, he offered a first edition copy of the seven-volume biography of Winston Churchill.

How did President Obama reciprocate you wonder?

The United States leader offered a Collector's Edition of 25 American Classic Films on DVD. A wonderful memorabilia of what America does best, the movies.

It is not known if the PM is an American movie aficionado. It is also not mentioned if the DVDs were in the European viewing format. The point about this example is that the press and the public perceived this gift exchange as unequal gift giving.

Before you take out your corporate credit card to input its number on a retailer's online website consider the following gift giving guidelines.

CHECK THE GIFT POLICIES ....

In recent years, because of newly uncovered corrupt practices, corporate gift giving must not be to obtain, retain or reward business. In government and international relations, gone are the days of coveted sports tickets, cruise vacations and expensive trinkets. These days, most governmental agencies and businesses have gift-giving and receiving policies.

In it, you will usually find the accepted nominal value of the gift. The gift value also applies to the price of tickets for entertainment, leisure or cultural activities.

Some companies choose to have a per occasion value while others make it an annual amount.

Canada Post Employee Gift policy
Gifts, Hospitality or Other Benefits: Employees must refuse gifts or other benefits, including benefits to family members, friends, or business associates, which could influence or be perceived to influence the employee's judgment. An employee may accept gifts or mementos with a nominal value of $100 if they are for legitimate business purposes, are appropriate to the business of both parties, are considered a normal business expense and do not impose a sense of obligation or result in any kind of special treatment for the donor.

When in doubt, call the HR department, theirs and/or yours to find out about gift compliance. It is better to be safe than sorry. Validate amounts and possible objections.

RESPECT COMPANY AND PERSONAL VALUES

Seek gifts that promote your company's values and appeal to the person's hobbies, activities and interests. Furthermore, take into account cultural diversity. For example, the traditional bottle of wine may be taboo in some cultures.

CONSIDER THE AFTER GIFT EFFECT

Where will the gift live after you offer it? How will it be used or stored? Yes, you want to be remembered along with your gift, but be careful of too much branding. A discreet logo on a small useful gift can be a gentle reminder while a huge logo on a trinket will be perceived as tacky and self-boosting.

SELECT APPROPRIATE GIFTS

Your gift should leave a positive and lasting impression not too personal and not too expensive. The average safe and compliant gift amount seems to be $25.

Appropriate gifts include:

- Desk and office accessories: a stylish pen, a water bottle or a USB key
- Travel accessories: an umbrella, a travel alarm clock or an international electric outlet adapter
- Perishable goods: treats, teas and plants
- Gift certificates for: the movies, the bookstore, or the local coffee shop
- Books on the recipient's hobby or passion
- Gift baskets of epicurean delights or snacks, an assortment of sweet treats and candies are especially appreciated by teams

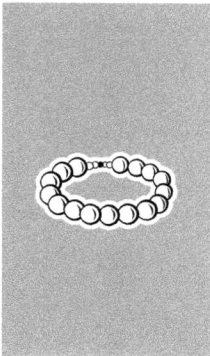

The safest business gift is a charity gift card. The receiver gets a gift card in person or via a virtual link. He then visits the website and enters the code on the card. He selects the charity of his choice to receive the amount indicated on the card. This option has the bonus of an exponential effect; a third party receives, and our world is better. Visit www.canadahelps.org for more information.

Keep a few staple gifts on hand. Pre-gifting will have you prepared when you just do not have the time to step out and shop.

Favourites include good-quality pens for clients and movie or bookstore gift certificates for colleagues.

PRESENT YOUR PRESENT

Wrap your gift to appeal to the eyes and for functionality, so that it is easy to open.

Always attach a personalized handwritten note to your gift. Short and sweet will do. "Happy holidays and best wishes for a successful year."

Choose an appropriate moment to offer your gift. Do not rush it. Add words to your presentation, "I really appreciate your business and am proud to count you as a client. Please accept this token of my appreciation."

KEEP TRACK OF GIFTS

It is a good idea to keep a gift registry of offered and received gifts with names, dates and occasions. This way, you will avoid offering duplicate gifts, and it will give you a memory aid to follow up with thank-you notes.

When exchanging gifts in the international business arena, it is a good idea to coordinate the gift giving with the recipient's visit coordinator. Communicate ahead and inform the coordinator of your gift selection. Also, take this opportunity, to find out if a similar object has been received during this tour. This will avoid offering duplicate gifts. Therefore, your recipient will not have to feign appreciation when he receives his fifth can of maple syrup during his Canadian tour.

NEVER OFFER CASH

Simply put, it could be perceived as bribery.

Avoid cultural blunders by seeking guidance from the visiting or hosting coordinator. Colors, objects and numbers may have different meanings in other parts of the world. Even the wrapping counts. You wouldn't want to offend a client with a simple ribbon, which has the wrong color.

| ACCEPTING A GIFT

When receiving a gift, take the time to connect to the person. Stop what you are doing. Give the bearer your undivided attention. Make eye contact. Smile. Open it, gently. Do not toss it aside.

The bearer wants to see your reaction. To me that is half the fun of giving.

Sincerely thank the giver for his/her thoughtfulness. "Thank you. That is very kind of you. I really appreciate the gesture."

Follow up with a thank-you note. Read how to write a thank-you note on the next page.

If you received a gift by courier, mail or a virtual link, thank the sender as soon as possible with a note or acknowledge receipt via email or a call and follow up with a thank-you note.

| DECLINING A GIFT

When you receive a gift that is not in line with your company's values, one that is too generous or too personal, you must decline it, immediately. Do not let it linger.

When offered a gift in person, speak with the person in private and explain why you cannot accept the gift. "Thank you for your gift. Because of our company's policy, the accepted gift amount or…I must decline it." If appropriate add, "I appreciate the thought."

When you receive an inappropriate gift via a delivery, return it to its sender, right away, with an explanation note. Document the incident and involve a witness, like HR.

Your note should clearly explain the reason why you are not accepting the gift. Stay professional and gracious.

Dear_____,

You really know me well. It is very thoughtful of you to offer me tickets to my favourite band's concert. I regret to inform you that my company's policy does not allow me to accept such a generous gift.

I really appreciate your thoughtfulness and look forward to serving you again very soon.

With kind appreciation,

Dear_____,

My company's gift policy is very strict. Due to the personal nature of your gift and for personal professional reasons, I must decline it.

I look forward to our continued business relationship.

Sincerely,

Make a copy of the note and the tracking slip. Keep them in a safe place, just in case the item does not make it back to its sender.

The next time that you interact with the sender, carry on as usual. Do not mention the gift gaffe.

	If the gift is more personal in nature or even romantic, respectfully state that for professional reasons, you cannot accept it.

If he/she mentions the gift and apologizes, graciously accept the apology and move on to the business at hand.

| OFFERING TO COLLEAGUES

When thinking of interoffice gift giving it may be an even stickier situation than giving to external clients. You certainly do not want to be sending the wrong message to the right person.

Gift giving in the workplace does not have specific rules. In fact, business etiquette does not require you to give gifts at work. It is an organizational custom. Observe your office's practices and when in doubt, to avoid making an intra-office faux pas, find out from a close colleague or HR.

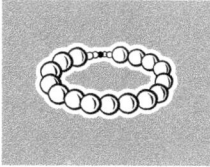

> When buying a gift for a workmate, foremost consider the message you want to convey to that person and not what you expect in return in the future.
>
> Your gift allocation should be based on your budget, your past relationship to that person, and their likes.

FOR YOUR BOSS

In most work environments, buying a gift for the boss is a bad idea. The reason is simple: It could be perceived as a quest for favours. The colour of Rudolph's famous nose is red, not brown. Let us keep your nose colour intact.

Your gift to the boss is doing a good job and meeting expectations all year round.

Should you wish to recognize your boss, there are a couple of ways to do it:

- Contribute or initiate a group gift by having all of your counterparts participate.

- A handwritten holiday greeting card is another simple, yet very effective, gesture that can go a long way in showing thankfulness. Keep it simple, to the point, and close with the season's wishes when appropriate.

FOR YOUR SUBORDINATES

Avoid perceptions of discrimination and favouritism by offering similar gifts of equal value to all. Although you may not expect it, the reality is your employees will compare.

Another popular option is a group gift such as a basket of sweet gourmet treats to be shared by all.

You can also opt to treat your entire department to a meal. Choose a restaurant where all in your group will be able to enjoy the food and the atmosphere.

While you are in gift-giving mode, you may also wish to single out a helpful colleague in another department. Offer that gift discreetly and away from the office during a lunch or coffee break.

Now for the tough part, what do you give? It is challenging enough finding that perfect gift for your loved ones, but what about for your cubicle mates, the ones you see Monday to Friday from nine to five?

Whether you participate in a Secret Santa, where employees randomly draw names for gift exchanging or you recognize one co-worker, buying for your boss and subordinates, regularly update your inner gift GPS. Make mental notes during water cooler talks. Listen for likes, hobbies, and collectibles.

GENERAL GIFT GIVING DO'S AND DON'TS ....

DO participate in organized gift giving; respect the guidelines and budget.

DON'T spend less or more than expected. *The Grinch* and *Richie Rich* are fictional characters, and their behaviours have no place in a civil office environment. Your boss knows how much you make. Based on the value of your gift, he/she may deduce that you are not very good at managing money or that he/she is paying you too much.

DO take the time to wrap the gift nicely and accompany it with a handwritten note. Slipping a gift receipt inside the box is also a good idea as it gives the receiver the opportunity to exchange it graciously.

DON'T buy gag, personal, or fragrant items. For cultural reasons, stay clear of alcohol. These gifts could offend, embarrass, or put you and the receiver in a very sticky situation.

DO acknowledge all gifts with a sincere thank you. Handwritten notes are always appropriate but not necessary when acknowledged face-to-face.

Should you receive an unexpected gift or card, remember, you do not have an obligation to reciprocate.

Acknowledge the gesture, say thank you, and offer your best wishes.

Do not lie about having forgotten that person's gift at home.

A good tip is to always have a couple of extra, more generic gifts for those surprise gifts.

SUMMARY

- Never underestimate the positive and lasting impression of the thank-you note. It is well worth the time and effort.
- The perfect gift is personal while not overstepping professional boundaries. It may involve research and coordination, especially in international relations.
- An intimate or overgenerous gift must be declined and returned.

Making your career vision come true does not stop here. It is a process that will be in constant evolution. When in doubt about how, to do or say, most of the time you will find the answers to your questions in this book. For all those other times when you are seeking solutions to sticky situations, I refer you to my maternal grandmother's words of wisdom. They are on the following, last pages, of this book.

NOT SO FAMOUS BUT DEFINITELY LAST WORDS

> **When in doubt, find out!**
>
> —Florina Salvas, my maternal grandmother

Now that you know how to: Take control of your first impressions, Dress for your client, Communicate correctly with technology, Participate in meetings meaningfully, Contribute to civility at work, Do not do lunch to eat and drink, Network to increase your net worth and Thank to be remembered, there will still be days when you will encounter sticky situations. Some of them will involve colleagues, others clients and even your superiors will stomp you with potentially awkward or embarrassing scenarios.

My story, that of a contemporary etiquette expert, is not one that could have been predicted. I grew up a lefty and like most of us, kind of gauche. I encountered many sticky situations. I stuck out and was noticed for the wrong reasons. Basically, I became an etiquette expert out of survival. With my new knowledge, I built the career of my dreams. If I can do it, you can too.

I vividly remember being marginalized. As a result, I wanted to find out how to blend in. I just wanted to fit in with the other 90% of the world that is right-handed. Fortunately for me, I had a grandmother that valued and was fascinated by how different people did different things.

Born in 1896, my maternal grandmother was not a very educated woman, but she was culturally intelligent. She was genuinely empathetic to others' way of doing things. She was fascinated by diversity at a time where it was not popular. She wanted to learn how others did what they did. She was never afraid to ask.

Through the years, as my professional career evolved from public relations, to retail, to human resources and onto training and development, I used my grandmother's wisdom and found out by asking questions. That same humility and curiosity should apply to the grey areas of your business activities. That is what business intelligence is all about; finding out and adapting.

Confidently know that there is never any harm in asking. Knock on the door of a trusted senior colleague. Walk down the hall to human resources. Call your host or the coordinator of the event. You have options.

After all, it is your responsibility to know how to do and say. My job is to give you the answers to make sure that you will be at your best.

You can always Ask Julie by visiting my website at etiquettejulie.com[33]. You can also exchange with others on my *Facebook* page[34] or on LinkedIn[35], keep the conversation going on the *Twitter* thread[36], or email me at julie@etiquettejulie.com.

Want to take it a step further? Whenever or wherever you need me, I will be there. I offer private coaching, webinars, customized workshops plus training activities for small, medium and large groups. I am always happy to travel to spread the word on etiquette as the ultimate confidence and credibility boost.

Before I say, "Au revoir," I leave you with a sticky situation survival kit, inspired by Louree Jefferson, Hotel Banquet Captain, of the Walt Disney World Double Tree resort [36].

Go to your odds and ends drawer or favourite dollar store to gather:

A penny: to remind you that you are lucky; you can create your own career vision.

An eraser: to remind you that you have a right to make mistakes.

A *Hershey's* kiss: to remind you that someone loves you.

A marble: just in case you lose yours.☺

A rubber band: to remind you to stretch and reach for your dreams.

A gold star: to remind you that I believe in you.

Keep your kit in a drawer or box and open it when necessary.

Good luck. Make your career vision come true!

Julie

Your dream career partner

[33] http://www.etiquettejulie.com
[34] https://www.facebook.com/EtiquetteJulieCanada?ref=hl
[35] https://www.linkedin.com/in/julieblaiscomeau
[36] https://twitter.com/EtiquetteJulie

INDEX FOR ACTIVITES, TEMPLATES & TUTORIALS

Julie Blais Comeau spent more than 20 years as an executive in corporate human resources, operations, training and development.

Her career has contributed to the employability of more than 5000 men and women.

She currently designs and conducts business etiquette workshops for crown corporations, colleges, universities, and private businesses. Her clients include engineering, law, accounting, federal government departments and IT companies where she also coaches in private sessions through the ranks: from recruits to CEOs.

After a harrowing and life-changing experience, which Julie shares in her first book, **ETIQUETTE: CONFIDENCE & CREDIBILITY**, she left her senior-level corporate job to start **Etiquette Julie**. She writes about contemporary business etiquette and also includes her own evolution in the business world as well as how she created her career in professional etiquette out of, "*Sheer necessity and a burning desire to empower others.*"

Julie has journeyed all the way from a self-described gauche-girl to a gaffe-proof teacher, and no one is better equipped to offer this training to help others excel in their careers.

A graduate of the world-renowned Protocol School of Washington, she is now in demand as an etiquette expert, writer, educator, and speaker. Julie's dynamic and down-to-earth way of teaching, combined with her extensive knowledge of all things etiquette also make her a perfect media contributor for today's digital and culturally diverse workplace. She appears regularly on *CBC Radio* and *TV, CTV* and has appeared on *Entertainment Tonight Canada*. Her bilingual blog column, *Sticky Situations* is featured in the *Huffington Post Canada* and *Québec*. Her views and opinions on etiquette have been quoted in many publications including *Reader's Digest* and *The Globe and Mail*.

With Julie's help, gone will be the professional *faux pas*!

To gaffe-proof your career, visit etiquettejulie.com[37], become a fan on *Facebook*[38] and follow her on *Twitter*[39] or ask julie@etiquettejulie.

---

[37] http://www.etiquettejulie.com
[38] https://www.facebook.com/EtiquetteJulieCanada
[39] https://twitter.com/EtiquetteJulie

www.ingramcontent.com/pod-product-compliance
Lightning Source LLC
Chambersburg PA
CBHW070903270326
41927CB00011B/2442